Sarvavyaapi Siksha

सर्वव्यापी शिक्षा

*Harmonizing Growth and Inclusion for
Every Child*

Diptii Karaambe & Ameya V Karrambe

Foreword by **Kim John Payne**
(Author of Simplicity Parenting)

ISBN
Paperback: 979-8-89186-819-9
Hardcase: 979-8-89233-755-7

"Sarvavyaapi Siksha: Harmonizing Growth and Inclusion for Every Child"

"Sarvavyaapi " means all-encompassing or holistic, reflecting the inclusive nature of the book's content, covering both Waldorf education principles and Curative Education insights.

"Siksha" translates to education, emphasizing the focus on educational practices and approaches discussed in the book.

"Harmonizing Growth" signifies the balance between nurturing a child's overall growth, encompassing physical, emotional, artistic, and intellectual aspects.

"Inclusion for Every Child" emphasizes the importance of an inclusive approach that addresses the needs of all children, including those with special needs.

This title aims to convey the book's core message of nurturing holistic growth while ensuring inclusivity and support for every child, making it relevant and appealing to the Indian market.

To truly know the world, look deeply within your own being;
to truly know yourself, take real interest in the world.

— Rudolf Steiner

Contents

Preface

Welcome to "Sarvavyaapi Siksha: Harmonizing Growth and Inclusion for Every Child" - a journey into the enriching world of Waldorf education and its transformative impact on children, families, and communities.

In this book, we embark on a compelling exploration of Waldorf education, a time-tested educational approach that goes beyond traditional academics to embrace the all-encompassing growth of every child. "Sarvavyaapi," meaning holistic or all-encompassing, reflects the heart of our discussions. We delve into the principles, practices, and experiences that make Waldorf education a unique and nurturing pathway for every child's development.

Waldorf education traces its roots to the visionary philosopher and educator Rudolf Steiner, who understood that education should not merely focus on intellectual growth but encompass physical, emotional, artistic, and spiritual dimensions. Steiner's profound insights and his philosophy of Anthroposophy lay the foundation for the Waldorf approach, emphasizing the uniqueness of each child and the importance of cultivating a love for learning.

In this book, we take a multi-dimensional approach, delving into various aspects of Waldorf education and how it harmonizes growth and inclusion for every child. We explore the role of imagination and play in learning, the significance of artistic expression, and the integration of rhythms and rituals into daily life.

Moreover, we address the importance of nurturing early childhood, with a focus on the home environment and the role of parents in the educational journey. We celebrate the art of Eurythmy, a unique form of movement that fosters creativity, self-expression, and social cohesion within the Waldorf community.

Inclusivity is a vital pillar of Waldorf education, and we devote chapters to understanding some special needs like Sensory Processing Disorder (SPD), ADHD, and autism spectrum disorder (ASD). We showcase the measures taken by Waldorf schools to create therapeutic environments that cater to the individuality of each child, ensuring that no child is left behind.

Additionally, we highlight the impact of Waldorf education on family life and values, emphasizing the harmonious connection between school and home. We explore how Waldorf principles enrich family traditions, nurture strong bonds, and cultivate lifelong learning mindsets for parents and children alike.

As we traverse these journey's, we embrace the cultural context of India, adapting the Waldorf approach to resonate with its diverse traditions and values. We understand the challenges and aspirations of fostering a Waldorf movement in this vibrant nation.

This book is a celebration of the essence of Waldorf education - an education that cherishes the magic of childhood, nurtures the development of well-rounded individuals, and fosters a sense of belonging and inclusivity. It is a testament to the transformative power of a holistic approach that recognizes the infinite potential within each child.

We hope that "Sarvavyaapi Siksha: Harmonizing Growth and Inclusion for Every Child" serves as a guiding light for parents, educators, and anyone passionate about embracing a holistic and inclusive education for the future generations. May it inspire a harmonious and compassionate world where every child's growth is cherished, and every heart finds its true expression.

With warm regards,

Diptii Karaambe & Ameya V Karrambe

Our highest endeavor must be to develop free human beings who are able of themselves to impart purpose and direction to their lives. The need for imagination, a sense of truth, and a feeling of responsibility – these three forces are the very nerve of education.

– Rudolf Steiner

Acknowledgements

Crafting a book is a profound labor of love, a journey that beckons the unwavering support and inspiration of many souls. As I stand at the culmination of "Sarvavyaapi Siksha: Harmonizing Growth and Inclusion for Every Child," my heart swells with humility and gratitude for the myriad hands that have woven this tapestry of knowledge.

Foremost, my gratitude unfurls like a boundless horizon towards Rudolf Steiner, the luminary whose visionary insights and profound philosophy of Anthroposophy laid the sacred cornerstone of Waldorf education. His wisdom continues to be the guiding light that has illuminated the path of countless educators, parents, and learners, bestowing lasting blessings upon children worldwide.

My heartfelt appreciation extends to a constellation of luminaries who have kindled the flames of inspiration on this arduous journey:

1. Kim John Payne, a global authority in the realms of Parenting and Waldorf Education, has been an unwavering guide on our journey. His invaluable coaching served as the bedrock that strengthened our dedication to the Waldorf philosophy, turning the initial hurdles our beloved child, Arnav, faced into stepping stones. His teachings and ongoing support continue to inspire us as we embark on a mission to share the gift of empowering parents to nurture their children.

2. Dr. Lakshmi Prasanna, our guide and teacher who truly inspires us every moment, She is a known Waldorf educator in India, whose boundless dedication to Waldorf education has been the wellspring of our motivation.

3. Sowmya Vikram, our guiding star during the most trying moments, a luminary in her own right, striding in the realms of special education, Waldorf Kindergarten teaching, and crafting.

4. Seshadri Desikan, Bindu Chowdhury, and Apeksha Chowdhury from Inodai Waldorf School in Mumbai. Their tireless dedication and unwavering enthusiasm have been our guiding light urging us towards the path of offering something back to our community.

5. Our beloved son Arnav, whose inquisitive spirit propelled us towards profound studies and brought us closer to our purpose.

6. Gratitude flows to Nilesh Jagad & to all the dedicated teachers who have been vital co- travellers on Arnav's educational odyssey.

7. Our esteemed parents, Vijay Karambe, Sandhya Karambe, Suhas Kambli, Smita Kambli, and all our other cherished family members.

8. To the parents and families who have embraced the Waldorf approach, I am deeply beholden for your openness and eagerness to contribute your experiences. Your narratives, entwined with the transformative magic of Waldorf education within family life, have enriched the very essence of this book.

9. Lastly, our deepest gratitude is reserved for the paramount luminary in our lives, our Guru and Spiritual Teacher, Dr. Aniruddha Joshi, affectionately known as Bapu. It is through his divine blessings and unwavering guidance that every facet of our journey has unfolded.

Special thanks are whispered to the Waldorf schools, the Anthroposophical Society India, Ira Waldorf Education, and the myriad communities in India and across the globe for their unwavering commitment to fostering inclusive and nurturing havens. Your dedication to embracing diversity and individuality shines as a beacon, illuminating the path for educational practices universally. We extend our sincere appreciation & credit to Freepik.com for their invaluable contribution to our project. Numerous images in the book have been meticulously crafted using assets from Freepik.com. Special recognition is also due to Suhas Jawkhedkar, a distinguished graphic designer based in Mumbai, who generously volunteered his expertise for this cause. Mr. Jawkhedkar, through his dedicated service, provided pro bono(voluntarily without payment) assistance in designing the artwork for us, demonstrating a commendable commitment to our shared mission.

To my friends and colleagues who have been unswerving sentinels, their unwavering support and motivation have been the cornerstones of strength.

A profound tribute is extended to the editorial team (Mydhili Mithra from Notion Press) and reviewers (Swapnil Shahu & Arshi Rakhangi) who have painstakingly sculped and polished this book, ensuring that its message resonates clearly with its readers.

Finally, to you, dear readers of "Sarvavyaapi Siksha: Harmonizing Growth and Inclusion for Every Child," I extend a heart brimming with gratitude for embarking on this voyage with me. May this book spark the flames of ardor for holistic education and kindle a world where every child is cherished, nurtured, and enveloped in the warm embrace of inclusion.

In closing, the birth of this book has been a collaborative labor of love. I am deeply honored to stand among a community of souls who believe ardently in the transformative alchemy of education. Your unwavering support and harmonious collaboration have translated this vision into a vibrant reality.

With the deepest wellspring of gratitude,

Ameya V Karrambe

Foreword

As I hold the bound pages of "Sarvavyaapi Siksha: Harmonizing Growth and Inclusion for Every Child" in my hands, I realize this isn't just another book; it's a beacon guiding us on a journey into the realm of holistic education, illuminated by the transformative light of Waldorf principles.

Education, the cornerstone of our future, lies at the heart of this book. "Sarvavyaapi Siksha" captures the essence of an educational paradigm that treasures childhood, fosters the flames of creativity, and honors the unique individuality of each and every child. It lays out the visionary wisdom of Rudolf Steiner, whose philosophy of Anthroposophy sowed the seeds for this revolutionary approach, transcending the confines of traditional learning.

This book explores the subtle layers of Waldorf education. Every chapter reveals facets of this all-encompassing philosophy, guiding us from the bedrock principles of Waldorf education to the nurturing of early childhood, the cultivation of creativity, and the healing of Eurythmy.

Inclusivity, a cornerstone of Waldorf education, is lovingly etched throughout this book. It exemplifies the commitment to embrace the diverse needs of each and every child. The Waldorf approach to children with special needs is tenderly and realistically portrayed, illustrating how individualized support and nurturing environments, when used wisely, can unlock the deep potential of every young learner.

The influence of Waldorf education extends far beyond the classroom, weaving into the tapestry of family life and values. This book beautifully connects the harmonious connection between home and school, nurturing strong familial bonds and sowing the seeds for a lifelong love of learning.

At its core, this book is a celebration of childhood itself - a time of enchantment, curiosity, and limitless potential. "Sarvavyaapi Siksha" isn't merely an invitation to comprehend Waldorf education; it is an invitation to rediscover the enchantment of childhood and to cherish the journey of growth and learning that every child embarks upon.

While you delve into in the pages, pause and take time to reflect the inspiration it offers, and acknowledge the significance of nurturing the complete child, nurturing a deep-seated passion for learning, and fostering an inclusive and compassionate society.

I extend my appreciation to the authors for presenting this enlightening approach to education. May this book find its way into the hearts and minds of its readers, and may its message ripple outward, further kindling a quiet revolution in education that celebrates the full potential of every child.

With warm regards,

Kim John Payne
Author- Simplicity Parenting

About Kim John Payne

Kim John Payne, an award-winning author, is dedicated to helping individuals voice the discomfort they feel amid the overwhelming new normal. With 27 years of experience as a school counselor, educator, and family consultant, he addresses a spectrum of issues, advocating for balanced, simple lives.

Payne has trained over 230 U.S. schools and consulted internationally, contributing to educational movements worldwide. As the Director of the Simplicity Project, he has trained global parenting coaches. Payne, the Founding Director of The Center for Social Sustainability, supports teachers, parents, and students globally.

Author of bestseller **"Simplicity Parenting,"** translated into 27 languages, Payne's media presence includes TV appearances on major networks and features in renowned publications. Residing in Ashfield, Massachusetts, he embodies a commitment to understanding and offering practical tools for navigating life's challenges amidst contemporary social issues.

Books by Kim John Payne
Simplicity Parenting
The Soul of Discipline
Games Children Play
The Minimalist Manifesto
The Social Inclusion Approach
Emotionally Resilient Tweens and Teens
Beyond Winning
Being at Your Best When Your Kids Are at Their Worst

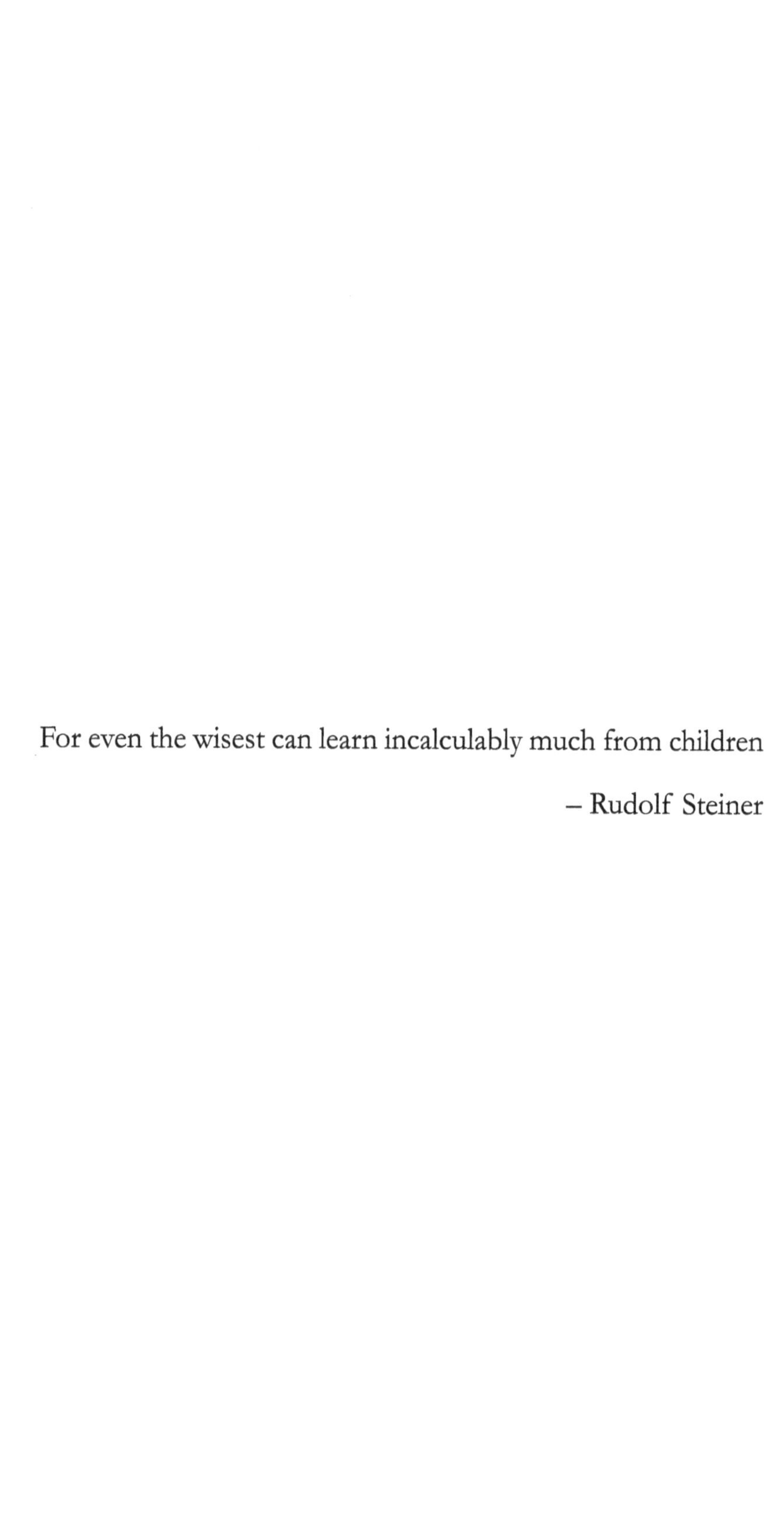

For even the wisest can learn incalculably much from children

– Rudolf Steiner

About this Book - Introduction

"Sarvavyaapi Siksha: Harmonizing Growth and Inclusion for Every Child" is an enlightening and comprehensive exploration of Waldorf education, offering a holistic approach to child development that embraces the uniqueness of each individual. The title itself, "Sarvavyaapi Siksha," meaning all-encompassing education, reflects the central theme of the book - to provide a nurturing and inclusive educational journey for every child.

The book begins by introducing readers to the foundational principles of Waldorf education, deeply rooted in the visionary insights of Rudolf Steiner and his philosophy of Anthroposophy. This sets the stage for understanding the overarching mission of Waldorf schools - to foster not only intellectual growth but also emotional, artistic, and spiritual development.

Throughout the chapters, the book delves into various aspects of Waldorf education, starting with the critical importance of early childhood nurturing. It emphasizes the role of parents as the child's first teachers, creating a Waldorf-inspired home environment, and fostering the child's imagination and play. The book further explores the Waldorf curriculum, with a focus on an artistic approach to learning and integrating academic subjects through thematic blocks, fostering creativity and critical thinking in children.

Rhythms and rituals hold a special place in Waldorf education, and the book beautifully portrays how celebrating festivals and seasons, as well as daily and weekly rhythms, create a harmonious and nurturing environment for children's well-being.

Inclusivity lies at the heart of Waldorf education, and the book also creates awareness the about special needs like Sensory Processing Disorder (SPD), ADHD, and Autism spectrum disorder (ASD). It highlights how Waldorf schools provide individualized support and therapeutic environments to cater to the diverse needs of every child, ensuring no child is left behind.

A fascinating chapter on Eurythmy - the art of movement in Waldorf education - showcases its significance in fostering creativity, self-expression, and social cohesion within the Waldorf community. Beyond the classroom, the book explores the impact of Waldorf education on family life and values, emphasizing the harmonious connection between school and home. It celebrates the unique journey of parents and children together in embracing Waldorf principles beyond the classroom.

To add depth and context, the book includes insights into the experiences of notable personalities who have been influenced by Waldorf education, illustrating its positive impact on individuals across various professions and life paths.

As the journey concludes, the book addresses the challenges faced by the Waldorf movement in becoming widespread globally. It celebrates the growth of Waldorf education while acknowledging the niche nature of this approach and the need for greater awareness and promotion.

"Sarvavyaapi Siksha: Harmonizing Growth and Inclusion for Every Child" stands as a beacon of knowledge and inspiration for parents, educators, and anyone passionate about embracing an all-encompassing and inclusive education for the future generations. The book embodies the essence of Waldorf education - a transformative approach that cherishes childhood, fosters well-rounded individuals, and embraces the diversity of every child with love and compassion.

Editor's Note on Gender Reference

In "Sarvavyaapi Siksha: Harmonizing Growth and Inclusion for Every Child," we have made a conscious effort to use gender-inclusive language to reflect our commitment to inclusivity and to create a welcoming environment for all readers. Throughout the book, we have strived to use gender-neutral terms and expressions, avoiding the unnecessary use of gender-specific pronouns whenever possible.

In education and literature, language plays a crucial role in shaping perceptions and attitudes. By using gender-inclusive language, we aim to promote an environment that values and respects the diversity of all individuals, irrespective of their gender identity or expression. Our intent is to foster a sense of belonging and acceptance for every reader, regardless of their background or experiences.

We understand that language is a continually evolving aspect of communication, and while we have endeavored to be as inclusive as possible, there may still be instances where traditional gendered language may inadvertently appear. We acknowledge this and remain committed to learning, growing, and adapting our language to better reflect the principles of inclusivity.

We hope that by adopting gender-inclusive language in this book, we contribute to a more equitable and inclusive educational landscape, one that values and celebrates the unique qualities and contributions of all individuals. Your feedback and insights are always appreciated as we strive to improve our language practices and create an ever-welcoming space for all readers.

With gratitude and dedication to the pursuit of inclusivity,

 Notion Press

Some day, when I have grown sufficiently, I shall attain that
which I am destined to attain

– Rudolf Steiner

Our Life, Our Work Our Child

In the year 2015, under the golden sun's warm embrace, Ameya and I embarked on a new chapter as we bound our lives together in marriage. Yet, our journey had commenced over a decade prior. For 10 long and beautiful years, we nurtured our love, sharing dreams that held a special place in our hearts. Among those cherished dreams, none shone brighter than our yearning to become parents. This dream took root, and its fruits began to blossom just two years into our wedded union.

One fateful May morning, our hopes swelled to the brink of fulfilment. A missed period, a home pregnancy test, and the enchanting word "positive" sent waves of joy rippling through our souls. The prospect of cradling new life in our arms filled us with an ineffable delight. Little did we know, the universe had a different path charted for us, one riddled with trials and tribulations.

A mere five days after that blissful revelation, a merciless, searing pain clutched my abdomen. In sheer anguish, I sought the immediate solace of a local doctor, my heart heavy with dread. It was here that I underwent an ultrasound, and its verdict painted a grim reality – an ectopic pregnancy. In the cruel hands of fate, an emergency operation became my sole lifeline, and my brush with death left me with an indelible gratitude for the precious gift of life.

It was in the shadow of this harrowing ordeal that we turned to our spiritual teacher for solace and counsel. His words of wisdom were a soothing balm for our wounded souls, a gentle reminder that even in the darkest trials, there lies a hidden purpose. A remarkable mentor, he also bore the title of a medical doctor, and he ushered us toward a beacon of hope – a renowned gynaecologist in the bustling city of Mumbai, a specialist in IVF treatments.

In the hands of this skilled practitioner, hope was rekindled, and our journey to parenthood was reimagined. We clung to the idea of natural conception, despite the shadow of a ruptured fallopian tube that loomed from the previous ectopic pregnancy. A single, resilient tube remained, and through it, we yearned for life's miracle to grace our lives.

After eight arduous months of patience and hope, destiny once more intervened. One restless night, around 11:30 PM, the ominous spectre of pain revisited my abdomen. My initial dismissals as mere gas-related discomfort was swiftly supplanted by a sense of foreboding. Come morning, at 6:00 AM, I awoke Ameya, my rock and anchor, with a dire revelation. The pain had intensified, mirroring the ordeal that had previously led to the ectopic pregnancy.

With unwavering resolve, Ameya rushed me to the hospital, confronting a familiar yet terrifying specter of ectopic pregnancy. A pregnancy test confirmed our worst fears, but beneath the surface, I knew this pain foretold a dire outcome. Urgently, we requested an ultrasound, but time seemed to stretch endlessly as the ultrasound doctor delayed their arrival, oblivious to the looming crisis.

By 8:00 AM, after two agonizing hours, the ultrasound doctor arrived, unveiling a shocking, life-or-death reality. My body was haemorrhaging internally, and peril hung heavy in the air. In a frantic dash against time, I was rushed to the operation theatre, while Ameya was left to grapple with the abyss of uncertainty. The grim message delivered by the medical staff echoed with a chilling finality – my chances of survival teetered at a precarious 50-50.

In those harrowing hours, the benevolence of the divine, the unwavering support of our spiritual mentor, and the tireless efforts of our medical team combined to pull me back from the precipice of despair. I emerged from this life-threatening crucible, my heart still burdened with grief, and my future an uncertain canvas.

Throughout this tumultuous journey, it was Ameya's unflinching faith and relentless support that kept the flicker of hope alive. We clung to one another, our love growing stronger with each heart-wrenching trial.

Following the shadow of the second ectopic pregnancy, we turned to the gynaecologist recommended by our spiritual guide. Three months later, we embarked on an IVF cycle, a beacon of hope on our path to parenthood. Miraculously, in the very first cycle, our prayers were answered. Arnav, our precious miracle baby, entered our lives, a testament to the unyielding strength of the human spirit, the power of unwavering love, and the profound impact of never surrendering to despair.

Arnav, our precious son, is the radiant light of our lives. Born in the aftermath of two perilous ectopic pregnancies, he embodies our miracle, an IVF baby, and the heart of our family. His arrival gifted us boundless joy and brimmed our hearts with an abundance of love.

Our introduction to the realm of Waldorf education was serendipitous, guided by a close family member who passionately extolled its nurturing and holistic approach. Captivated by this philosophy, we enrolled Arnav in a Waldorf-inspired kindergarten when he was just 2.5 years old. From the very moment he crossed the threshold into that warm, loving environment, we knew that this decision was the right one for our cherished child.

As Arnav's parents, my husband Ameya and I were steadfast in our commitment to provide him with the very best upbringing. However, the unexpected upheavals brought about by the COVID-19 pandemic relegated our young one to the confines of our home, a situation that weighed heavily on his spirit. The loss of social interactions and the impact on his overall well-being were evident, and we knew we needed to take action.

When Arnav's long-awaited school journey finally commenced, we harboured hopes that the nurturing embrace of Waldorf education would ease his transition. Yet, we faced unexpected challenges as his exuberant hyperactivity emerged as a formidable obstacle. Struggling to fit into the school setting, he sometimes resorted to hitting, biting, and scratching, not only fellow students but even the teachers. Circle time, once an essential classroom ritual, became a strenuous exercise for him, as he battled to sit still and participate like his peers.

As parents, witnessing our spirited child grapple with such turbulent times was heart-wrenching. It was clear that we needed to advocate for him, just as we had done throughout our arduous journey to parenthood. Arnav's hyperactivity presented a unique challenge for the school, and instead of the support we had hoped for, we found ourselves mired in accusations that he was imitating negative behaviour from our home.

As parents, the weight of these accusations bore heavily on our hearts. We knew, without a shadow of a doubt, that we had fostered a loving and supportive home environment. It was a devastating blow to our spirits to feel judged and held responsible for Arnav's struggles in the school environment.

Amidst the shadows of uncertainty and the crucible of adversity, we turned to the guiding philosophy of Waldorf education for solace and inspiration. We recognized that Arnav's hyperactivity was an integral part of his unique personality. Instead of seeking to suppress it, we embraced the challenge of channelling his boundless energy in a positive direction.

Our commitment to Waldorf education deepened as we delved deeper into its profound principles. I embarked on a transformative journey to Chennai to attend IRA Module 1 with Dr. Lakshmi Prasanna, a journey that marked my first solo travel in 34 years. The meeting with Dr. Lakshmi Prasanna ushered in a new beginning, a profound exploration of the path of Waldorf education.

As parents, Ameya and I held a steadfast investment in Arnav's growth and development. We recognized the importance of providing an environment that celebrated his uniqueness and catered to his individual needs. In the wake of challenges faced in his previous school, we resolved to take action, ensuring that Arnav's educational journey would be imbued with love, care, and holistic development.

With hearts brimming with hope, we embarked on a quest to find the perfect educational fit for our spirited child. Our search led us to the bigger Waldorf School, where we felt an instant connection. The school's philosophy seamlessly resonated with our beliefs, and it became clear that this was the ideal place for Arnav to flourish.

Upon our arrival at the bigger Waldorf School, we were embraced with open arms and warm hearts. The teachers and staff displayed a genuine commitment to understanding and supporting Arnav's unique individuality. They dedicated time to observe his strengths and challenges, tailoring their approach to suit his specific needs.

Arnav's journey through the bigger Waldorf School has been nothing short of transformative. As parents, we witness the nurturing environment and the emphasis on creativity and play bringing out the best in him. What was once viewed as a challenge – his hyperactivity – was now embraced as an opportunity for growth and self-expression.

In a curriculum that celebrates the arts and encourages boundless imagination, Arnav's spirit is thriving. He enthusiastically engages in artistic activities and free-spirited movement, channelling his exuberance positively and expressing himself with unbridled joy.

While our journey with Arnav continues, it remains a testament to the extraordinary power of love and resilience. It is a testament to the transformative influence of Waldorf education on our lives. As we navigate this path together, our hearts are brimming with hope and gratitude for the opportunity to nurture our son's potential, and celebrate the radiant uniqueness that defines Arnav.

Arnav's journey is a testament to the boundless strength of a parent's love and the profound impact of finding the right educational approach for a child. Amidst the bustling city of Mumbai, where life races at a demanding pace, we find solace in the guiding light of Waldorf education, illuminating our son's path toward growth and self-discovery. Each passing day sees Arnav's spirit shining ever brighter, and we stand proudly as his parents, steadfastly supporting his quest for excellence, embracing his spirited nature, and fostering the values of Waldorf education within our family's remarkable journey.

With profound gratitude and unwavering dedication to the pursuit of excellence,

Diptii Karaambe

Embarking on a Quest: Navigating Challenges, Unearthing Discoveries!

Our odyssey into the world of Waldorf education began when our son, Arnav, was just 2.5 years old. It was a time filled with curiosity, excitement, and the promise of a bright future. This was before the cloud of Covid-19 had settled, and we were embarking on a quest to find the right school for our beloved child.

One sunny Monday morning, we received a call from one of the best schools in the suburbs of Mumbai. The news filled us with anticipation and joy, and we eagerly accepted the invitation for an interview. The school boasted beautiful aesthetics, and its lush green playground seemed like a child's paradise. As we arrived and joined the queue of parents, we couldn't help but notice something unusual. Arnav, being his vibrant and energetic self, couldn't sit still. He began exploring his surroundings, his curiosity boundless, while the other children were calm and composed. Their parents encouraged them to remain seated, creating a stark contrast.

A stern lady approached us, urging us to control Arnav's exuberance. We did our best, but his spirit was uncontainable. Time passed, and we were summoned to the principal's office, where we were offered tea and coffee. It was during this meeting that a profound question was posed to us: "What is your income?" I hesitated but eventually disclosed our income range. To our surprise, Arnav's admission was promptly confirmed, and we were asked to pay the fees without delay.

However, something didn't feel quite right. We left the school, uncertain about the path that lay ahead. While the school had received accolades, we believed that a child's formative years are critical to their future, and this school might not align with our aspirations.

That's when we discovered a Waldorf School, an educational institution with a difference. As we visited the new premise the school was shifting to in Andheri East, things were being made ready yet, Diptii, my wife, was introduced to Waldorf education, a moment that would change our lives forever. Meanwhile, I was busy playing with Arnav and missed the discussion. However, Diptii's enthusiasm was infectious. The school's philosophy resonated deeply with her, and she was convinced that this was the right place for our child. This was a Waldorf school, and though I had some knowledge of this method from my Train the Trainer program for adults, I had no idea it would soon become a shared passion for us.

The very next day, one of our acquaintance informed us about a Waldorf Kindergarten nearby our house which they had started, just a 10-minute drive away. We wholeheartedly agreed, and our Waldorf journey began. We enrolled in the Nearby school/kindergarten as the location was nearby and the fees were lesser.

We started with the Waldorf kindergarten, an institution that our acquaintance had initiated nearby to our house. In the initial days, Diptii accompanied Arnav, waiting in the school's cozy reception area, typical of Waldorf schools. Arnav, being a social and exuberant child, quickly adjusted. The school soon informed us that Diptii need not accompany Arnav any longer.

However, there was a catch. Arnav didn't like sitting in class, participating in circle time, or conforming to traditional norms. He was always on the move, preferring outdoor activities. The school suggested that his boundless energy should be directed towards outdoor play. So, we did just that. We also started taking him to the beach every day, a recommendation from the school.

Despite these efforts, challenges persisted. Diptii, a celebrity chef who was running her steamed Modak business, and I, a working professional, were both engaged in demanding commitments. Arnav may have felt neglected during these times.

I dropped him off at school one day, and the principal expressed concerns. He urged us to meet them to address these issues, but our immediate response was delayed due to Diptii's professional commitments.

When we finally met with the school, we were confronted with the school's struggles in managing Arnav's behaviour. They suggested that we should consult an occupational therapist for Arnav and offered to recommend one.

In light of Arnav's age, we decided that it was too early for occupational therapy. We believed he might be struggling with the transition due to his young age. We discussed this with the school, and they agreed to re-enroll him once he turned 3 years old. However, my worry lingered.

Eventually, we decided to seek the opinion of a developmental pediatrician. She assessed Arnav and assured us that he was a normal child with only minor developmental delays. To address these, we devised a home routine, and we employed an occupational therapist who conducted sessions at our residence for a period of 7-8 months.

After Arnav turned 3, we decided to reintroduce him to school. However, Diptii was reluctant to send him back to the same school.

She believed that the previous school's treatment towards us, as parents, had not been appropriate. In search of a new solution, Diptii even collected the school admission form from a bigger known Waldorf School in Andheri East which we had visited earlier before enrolling him in the acquaintance's school. But, after speaking with one of the school's founders, decided to continue at the same acquaintance school due to Arnav's young age. So, we returned to the same school.

The first three months were uneventful, but afterward, we began receiving complaints from the school once more. They recommended an occupational therapist, but this one was located quite far from our residence. Despite Arnav's reluctance, we decided to send him for occupational therapy, trusting that it was for his benefit.

One day, Arnav fell asleep on the way to Occupational Therapy. When the occupational therapy session venue arrived, Diptii tried to wake him. Arnav, now awake, looked at the session venue and began to cry, claiming that the OT teachers had hit him. He demanded that Diptii accompany him to the session, and she complied. During the session, she tactfully questioned the assistant, who reluctantly admitted that they sometimes hit Arnav lightly as a response to his misbehavior. Upon learning of this, Diptii decided to immediately discontinue these sessions.

Distressed by the ongoing struggles, we sought guidance from our spiritual teacher, who also happens to be a medical doctor by profession. He recommended consulting a well-known behavioral pediatrician. During our visit, the pediatrician assured us that Arnav was perfectly normal but noted that his heightened intelligence for his age might be causing anxiety. She recommended continuing occupational therapy and directed us to an OT therapist closer to our residence.

As Arnav began sessions with the new OT therapist, the challenges at school showed no signs of abating. It had become evident that the school was ill-equipped to manage Arnav's particular challenges, and we questioned our own decisions.

During this time, I encouraged Diptii to explore the Waldorf system and gain a deeper understanding. It was a significant turning point when Diptii travelled to Chennai alone to attend the IRA Teacher Training Workshop. There, she crossed paths with Dr. Laxmi Prasanna, who became our guiding star. Dr. Prasanna introduced us to Sowmya Vikram, an expert in working with special needs children, who was currently based in Mumbai. Alongside these mentors, Kim John Payne, the founder of Simplicity Parenting, provided invaluable coaching to tackle this difficult time.

Emboldened by this newfound support network, we took a daring step and decided to approach the Big Known Waldorf School in Andheri East which we had approached earlier, candidly sharing our challenges and the difficulties we were experiencing with Arnav. The mentors and founders of the school displayed remarkable compassion, actively listening to our concerns and accepting responsibility for Arnav's well-being. Arnav was enrolled in the new school, and we met Arnav's new teacher who was an experienced Waldorf teacher with a kind soul. She assured us that she felt lucky to have Arnav in her class. This moment felt nothing short of magic, and our entire perspective underwent a profound transformation.

This experience led me to realize that there must be countless parents navigating similar challenges, desperately seeking guidance while remaining unaware of the potential transformative power of Waldorf Education. It was during this realization that the idea of spreading awareness about this remarkable system and sharing our journey with other parents began to take shape.

Diptii encouraged me to attend the IRA training as well, and though I initially hesitated, my perspective transformed from the very very first day of training at IRA in Chennai. I realized that IRA was a unique space where the focus was solely on self-discovery and growth. Inspired by this, I decided to co-author a book with Diptii, with the aim of introducing the beauty of Waldorf Education to parents across India.

"Sarvavyaapi Siksha" is our endeavour to raise awareness about this beautiful system and share the transformative experiences we witnessed, not only in Arnav but also within ourselves. Our journey, characterized by challenges and magical discoveries, has motivated us to unveil the profound potential of Waldorf Education to others.

With profound gratitude,

Ameya V Karrambe

Unveiling Waldorf Magic: A Journey into Educational Enchantment!

Waldorf education is a unique and holistic approach to education that was founded by Rudolf Steiner in the early 20th century. The philosophy is based on the belief that every child is a unique individual with their own gifts and potential. Waldorf education seeks to nurture and develop the whole child - body, mind, and spirit - through a balanced and comprehensive curriculum. In this introduction, we will explore the core principles of Waldorf education and its emphasis on creativity, imagination, and the arts.

Waldorf education is a holistic and innovative approach to education that places the child at the center of the learning process. Developed by Rudolf Steiner in the early 20th century, this philosophy is founded on the belief that each child is a unique individual with their own gifts and potential. Unlike traditional education systems that focus solely on academic achievement, Waldorf education seeks to nurture and develop the whole child - body, mind, and spirit.

At the heart of Waldorf education is the recognition that children undergo distinct developmental stages, each requiring different approaches to learning. The curriculum is thoughtfully designed to meet the specific needs and capacities of children at various ages, fostering a natural and harmonious progression in their growth.

One of the core principles of Waldorf education is the value placed on imagination and play in learning. Young children are encouraged to engage in unstructured play, imaginative games, and creative storytelling. Such activities not only stimulate cognitive development but also promote emotional intelligence and social skills, as children learn to cooperate and communicate with one another.

The arts also hold a prominent place in Waldorf education. Music, painting, drawing, drama, and handwork are integrated into the curriculum, fostering creativity and self-expression. The arts are seen not only as avenues for developing skills but also as means of cultivating beauty, grace, and an appreciation for the world's wonders.

Rhythm and routine are essential elements of Waldorf education. Daily and weekly rhythms create a sense of predictability and security for children, supporting their well-being and helping them to engage more fully in their studies. The rhythm of the day, with its mix of academic lessons, artistic activities, and outdoor play, ensures a balanced and enriching experience for the child.

Teachers in Waldorf schools play a unique and vital role in the educational process. They are seen as guides and mentors, rather than mere instructors, and they strive to build strong, caring relationships with their students. Teachers observe and understand each child's individuality, tailoring their teaching methods to suit their diverse learning styles and needs.

Waldorf education extends beyond the classroom, encompassing the home and family life. Parents are encouraged to actively participate in their child's education, with the understanding that the home environment plays a significant role in shaping a child's development. This partnership between parents and teachers creates a sense of community and shared responsibility for the child's growth and well-being.

In this effort of introducing Waldorf education through Sarvavyaapi Siksha, we will explore the principles, practices, and benefits of this enriching educational philosophy. From nurturing creativity and imagination to fostering a lifelong love of learning, Waldorf education provides a nurturing and supportive environment in which children can thrive and discover their true potential. Through its holistic approach, Waldorf education aims to produce not just academically capable individuals, but also well-rounded, compassionate, and socially responsible human beings ready to contribute meaningfully to the world.

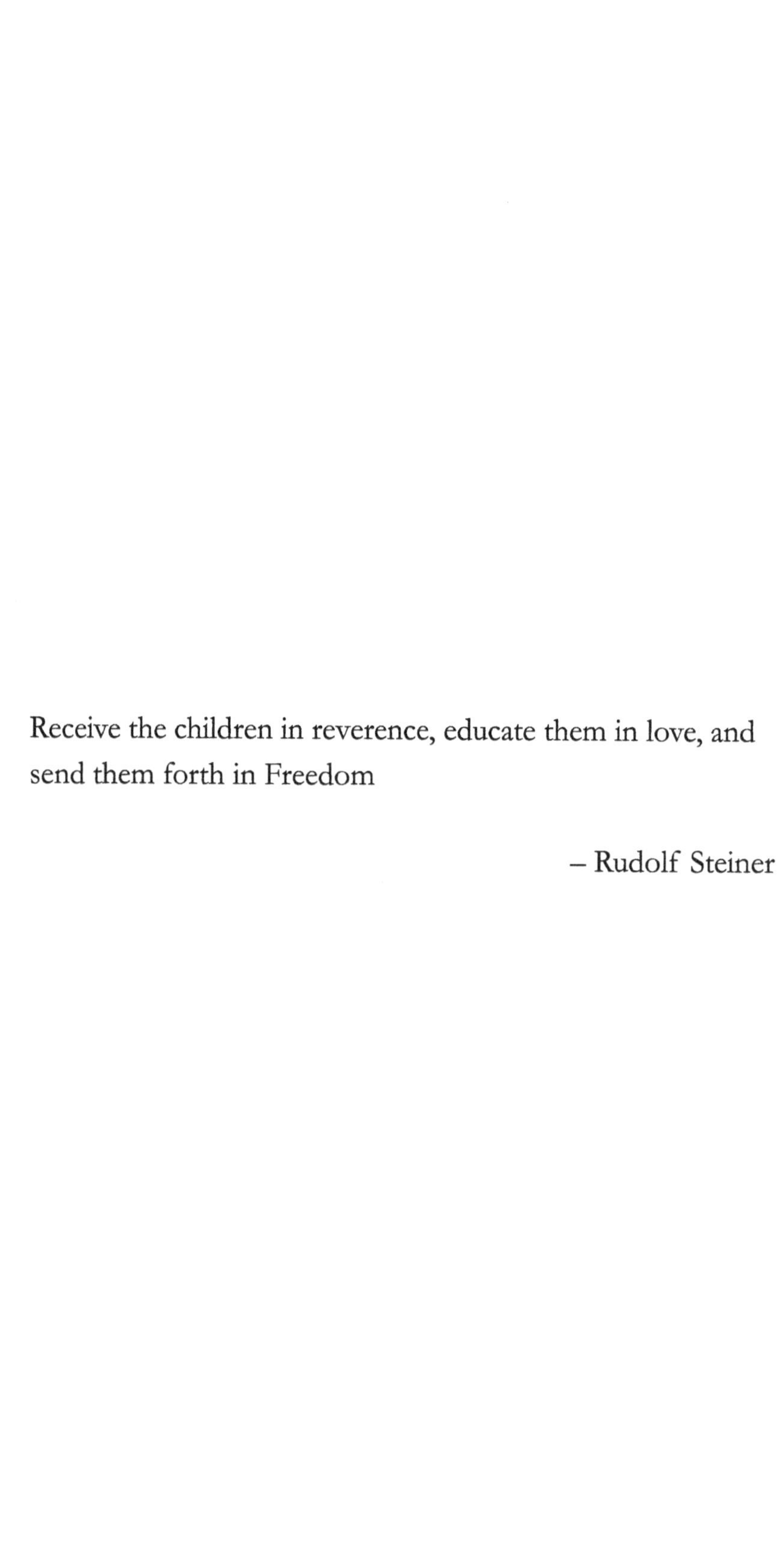

Receive the children in reverence, educate them in love, and send them forth in Freedom

– Rudolf Steiner

Rudolf Steiner's Influence on Waldorf Education

Rudolf Steiner, an Austrian philosopher, scientist, and educator, is the visionary behind Waldorf education. His profound influence on the development of this educational philosophy is the cornerstone of its principles and practices. Steiner's insights and beliefs laid the foundation for a holistic approach to education that embraces the development of the whole child - intellectually, emotionally, and spiritually.

In the early 20th century, Steiner was approached by Emil Molt, the owner of the Waldorf-Astoria Cigarette Factory in Stuttgart, Germany, to create a school for the children of the factory workers. Steiner accepted the challenge and presented his ideas for a progressive and transformative educational system. In 1919, the first Waldorf school was established, and it became the first embodiment of Steiner's vision.

Steiner's philosophy, known as Anthroposophy, is at the core of Waldorf education. Anthroposophy is a spiritual and philosophical belief system that seeks to understand the human being and the spiritual world through direct spiritual experience and observation. Steiner believed that each human being is a spiritual being with a unique individuality, and education should respect and nurture this individuality.

One of the key aspects of Steiner's influence on Waldorf education is his concept of the "septennials." He recognized that children go through distinct developmental stages approximately every seven years, and the curriculum and teaching methods should align with these stages to support the child's natural growth and learning.

Steiner also emphasized the importance of imagination and play in education. He understood that young children learn best through imaginative play and creative activities. This insight is reflected in the Waldorf kindergarten and early elementary years, where play and artistic activities are central to the curriculum.

Another significant aspect of Steiner's influence is the integration of the arts into the curriculum. He believed that the arts nourish the soul and spirit of the child and should be an essential part of education. In Waldorf schools, children engage in a wide range of artistic activities, including music, painting, drawing, drama, and handwork.

Additionally, Steiner emphasized the importance of a balanced and holistic education that includes not only intellectual development but also emotional, social, and spiritual growth. He believed that education should foster a love of learning and a sense of wonder and curiosity about the world.

Steiner's legacy lives on in Waldorf education, as his insights continue to guide and inspire educators worldwide. His vision of education as a means of nurturing the whole child and preparing them to become creative, compassionate, and responsible individuals is at the heart of Waldorf schools' educational mission. Today, Waldorf education remains true to Steiner's original principles while also adapting to meet the needs and challenges of the modern world.

Rudolf Steiner's lectures on Education

Rudolf Steiner delivered numerous lectures on education throughout his life, sharing his profound insights and vision for a transformative approach to teaching and learning. These lectures have become an invaluable resource for educators and parents interested in understanding the principles and practices of Waldorf education.

The key themes and topics found in Steiner's lectures on education:

1. **The Developmental Stages of Childhood:** Steiner emphasized the importance of understanding the distinct developmental stages that children go through, which he referred to as the "septennials." He believed that education should align with these stages to support the child's natural growth and development.

2. **The Role of Imagination:** Steiner stressed the significance of imagination and creative play in early childhood education. He understood that young children learn best through imaginative

play and storytelling, and this insight is reflected in the Waldorf kindergarten curriculum.

3. **The Importance of Art and Handwork:** Steiner believed that the arts nourish the soul and spirit of the child. He advocated for the integration of artistic activities, such as music, painting, drawing, drama, and handwork, into the curriculum to foster creativity and self-expression.

4. **Holistic Education:** Steiner emphasized the need for a balanced and holistic education that addresses not only intellectual development but also emotional, social, and spiritual growth. He believed in nurturing the whole child - body, mind, and spirit.

5. **Understanding the Individuality of Each Child:** Steiner recognized that each child is a unique individual with their own gifts and potential. He stressed the importance of respecting and nurturing the individuality of each student in the educational process.

6. **The Role of the Teacher:** Steiner saw teachers as guides and mentors rather than mere instructors. He believed that teachers should build strong, caring relationships with their students and strive to understand their individual needs and abilities.

7. **The Relationship between Education and Society:** Steiner believed that education plays a vital role in shaping the future of society. He envisioned education as a means of cultivating creative and responsible individuals who can contribute positively to the world.

Steiner's lectures on education have had a profound impact on the development of Waldorf education and continue to inspire educators around the world. His vision for education as a transformative and holistic process, grounded in the understanding of the developmental needs of children, remains at the heart of Waldorf schools' educational mission. Through his lectures, Steiner left a lasting legacy that continues to shape and enrich the lives of countless children and families.

Rudolf Steiner gave a significant number of lectures on education throughout his life. He was a prolific speaker and writer, and his lectures on education are an essential part of his contributions to the field of pedagogy. While it is challenging to provide an exact number due to the vastness of his work, it is estimated that Steiner delivered over **6,000 lectures** during his lifetime.

Among these numerous lectures, a substantial portion is dedicated to education and the principles of Waldorf education. These lectures were delivered to teachers, parents, and the general public and were often given as part of educational conferences or teacher training courses.

Steiner's lectures on education cover a wide range of topics, including child development, the role of the teacher, the curriculum, the importance of the arts, and the integration of spirituality in education. His insights and ideas continue to be studied and discussed by educators and scholars, and they serve as the foundation for Waldorf education and other educational movements inspired by his work.

Steiner's lectures on education have been compiled into various books and publications, making them accessible to a broader audience and ensuring that his ideas continue to inspire and inform educators around the world. His vision of education as a transformative and holistic process, rooted in a deep understanding of the needs of the child, has had a lasting impact and continues to shape educational practices and philosophies to this day.

Rudolf Steiner's lectures on Curative Education

Rudolf Steiner gave several lectures on curative education, also known as special education or remedial education, during his lifetime. Curative education is an approach that addresses the individual needs of children and individuals with developmental challenges, disabilities, or special needs. Steiner's lectures on this topic laid the groundwork for what is now known as "curative education" and have been influential in shaping the approach used in Waldorf schools and other educational settings.

In his lectures on curative education, Steiner emphasized the importance of understanding the unique individuality of each child and tailoring the educational approach to meet their specific needs. He believed that every child has their own developmental journey and that educators should approach each child with compassion, patience, and a deep understanding of their strengths and challenges.

Steiner's insights on curative education extended beyond the academic realm. He stressed the significance of fostering a nurturing and supportive environment that includes not only intellectual development but also emotional, social, and spiritual growth. He believed that a holistic approach is essential to support the overall well-being and growth of the child.

One of the key aspects of Steiner's approach to curative education is the belief in the healing power of art and creativity. He emphasized the therapeutic benefits of artistic activities, such as painting, music, movement, and drama, in supporting the development and healing of individuals with special needs. These artistic activities were incorporated into the curative education curriculum to foster self-expression, build confidence, and enhance social skills.

Steiner's lectures on curative education provided valuable insights into understanding and supporting children and individuals with special needs. His approach focused on recognizing the unique gifts and potential of each individual, fostering their growth and development in a way that respects and celebrates their individuality.

Today, curative education is an essential component of many Waldorf schools and other educational institutions. Steiner's contributions to this field continue to shape the way educators and caregivers approach special needs education, emphasizing empathy, creativity, and a deep respect for the dignity and potential of every individual.

It is important that we discover an educational method where people learn to learn and go on learning their whole lives

– Rudolf Steiner

The Foundations of Waldorf Education

"The essence of education is to help a person find their own way to what is true, beautiful, and good."

— Rudolf Steiner

The Foundations of Waldorf Education are rooted in the philosophical and educational principles developed by Rudolf Steiner. These foundations provide the framework for the unique and holistic approach that defines Waldorf education. Let's explore some of the key elements that form the bedrock of this educational philosophy:

1. **Anthroposophy:** At the core of Waldorf education is Anthroposophy, Steiner's spiritual and philosophical belief system. Anthroposophy seeks to understand the human being and the spiritual world through direct spiritual experience and observation. In Waldorf education, Anthroposophy informs the understanding of child development, the role of the teacher, and the design of the curriculum.

2. **The Unique Individuality of Each Child:** Waldorf education recognizes that each child is a unique individual with their own gifts and potential. Teachers strive to understand and honor the individuality of each student, creating a learning environment

that meets their specific needs and supports their growth and development.

3. **Holistic Development:** Waldorf education aims to nurture the whole child - body, soul, and spirit. The curriculum is designed to address not only intellectual development but also emotional, social, and spiritual growth. Artistic activities, movement, and handwork are integrated into the curriculum to foster creativity, self-expression, and a sense of well-being.

4. **Developmental Stages:** Steiner's concept of "septennials" recognizes distinct developmental stages that children go through approximately every seven years. Waldorf education aligns its curriculum and teaching methods with these stages to support the child's natural growth and learning.

5. **Importance of Imagination and Play:** In the early years of Waldorf education, there is a strong emphasis on imaginative play and storytelling. Children are encouraged to engage in unstructured play and creative activities, fostering a love of learning and a rich inner life.

6. **Rhythms and Routines:** Rhythms and routines play a significant role in Waldorf education. Daily and weekly rhythms create a sense of predictability and security for children, supporting their well-being and engagement in learning

7. **Arts and Handwork:** The arts hold a prominent place in Waldorf education. Music, painting, drawing, drama, and handwork are integrated into the curriculum, fostering creativity and self-expression.

8. **Role of the Teacher:** In Waldorf education, teachers are seen as guides and mentors. They seek to build strong, caring relationships with their students, understanding their individual needs and supporting their learning journeys.

These foundations collectively form the basis of Waldorf education, shaping an educational philosophy that celebrates the unique potential of each child, fosters a love of learning, and prepares students to become well-rounded, compassionate, and socially responsible individuals. Through its holistic approach and emphasis on the development of the whole child, Waldorf education aims to nurture lifelong learners who are well-prepared to navigate the complexities of the modern world with wisdom, creativity, and empathy.

Anthroposophy, the spiritual and philosophical belief system developed by Rudolf Steiner, evolved over the course of Steiner's life through a process of deep spiritual inquiry, study, and practical application. The evolution of Anthroposophy can be traced through several key phases:

•   **Early Life and Philosophical Studies:** Rudolf Steiner was born in 1861 in what is now Croatia. He studied philosophy, literature, and natural sciences at the University of Vienna and later became involved in the Theosophical Society. Steiner's early interests and studies laid the groundwork for his later spiritual explorations.

•   **Spiritual Experiences and Theosophical Influence:** In the late 19th century, Steiner began to have profound spiritual experiences and insights. He became associated with the Theosophical Society and worked closely with its leaders, Helena Blavatsky and Annie Besant. During this time, he developed his clairvoyant capacities and deepened his understanding of spiritual realities.

- **Break with Theosophy:** Steiner eventually broke away from the Theosophical Society due to differences in philosophical and spiritual perspectives. He felt the need to develop his own spiritual path, which led to the formulation of Anthroposophy as a distinct belief system and spiritual worldview.

- **Development of Anthroposophy:** From the early 20th century onwards, Steiner began to articulate his spiritual insights and philosophical concepts more systematically. He delivered thousands of lectures and wrote numerous books on topics ranging from education and agriculture to medicine and spiritual development. These writings and lectures formed the basis of Anthroposophy and its application in various fields of life.

- **Founding of the Waldorf School:** One of the significant practical applications of Anthroposophy was the founding of the first Waldorf school in 1919 at Stuttgart, Germany. The Waldorf school aimed to implement Steiner's educational principles and foster a holistic approach to child development.

- **Expansion and Influence:** Steiner's ideas gained popularity, and Anthroposophy began to spread internationally. Anthroposophical communities, schools, and institutions emerged in various countries, each applying the principles of Anthroposophy in different fields, such as education, agriculture, medicine, and the arts.

- **Continuing Development:** After Steiner's death in 1925, Anthroposophy continued to evolve through the work of his followers and colleagues. Anthroposophical societies and organizations were established to carry forward Steiner's work, promote research, and foster collaboration in various areas of life.

Today, Anthroposophy remains a living and evolving spiritual and philosophical movement. Its impact can be seen in the continued growth of Waldorf education, biodynamic agriculture, Anthroposophical medicine, and various other fields. The principles of Anthroposophy continue to inspire individuals and communities seeking to integrate spirituality, creativity, and practical wisdom into their lives and work.

Anthroposophy has a presence in India, where it has inspired various initiatives and communities across different domains.

Key aspects of Anthroposophy's influence in India:

- **Waldorf Education:** One of the most prominent expressions of Anthroposophy in India is the presence of Waldorf schools. These schools follow the educational principles and practices inspired by Rudolf Steiner's insights. Waldorf education in India emphasizes holistic development, artistic expression, and a child-centered approach. Several Waldorf schools have been established in different cities, offering a unique and nurturing learning environment.

- **Biodynamic Agriculture:** Anthroposophy has also influenced biodynamic agriculture in India. Biodynamic farming is a holistic and sustainable agricultural approach that incorporates spiritual perspectives on farming practices. There are biodynamic farms and initiatives in India that follow these principles and aim to promote ecological balance and environmental stewardship.

- **Anthroposophical Medicine:** The principles of Anthroposophy have also found application in alternative and holistic healthcare practices in India. Anthroposophical medicine integrates conventional medical knowledge with spiritual insights, focusing on the whole person's well-being, including physical, emotional, and spiritual aspects.

- **Anthroposophical Organizations:** India is home to several anthroposophical organizations and study centers that promote and disseminate the ideas of Rudolf Steiner. These organizations host lectures, workshops, and conferences on various Anthroposophical topics, fostering a community of like-minded individuals interested in holistic education, spirituality, and sustainable living.

- **Artistic and Cultural Expression:** Anthroposophy's emphasis on creativity and artistic expression is reflected in various artistic endeavors in India. There are Anthroposophical initiatives that focus on artistic activities, such as painting, music, drama, and eurythmy, as well as cultural events that celebrate creativity and spiritual exploration.

- **Spiritual and Philosophical Inquiry:** Anthroposophy has also influenced spiritual and philosophical exploration in India. Individuals and groups interested in spiritual development, meditation, and esoteric studies have drawn inspiration from the spiritual insights of Rudolf Steiner.

It is important to note that the application and expression of Anthroposophy in India may vary across different regions and communities. Anthroposophy, as a spiritual and philosophical belief system, seeks to address the individual needs and contexts of each culture and community it touches. As such, its influence in India is characterized by a diverse range of initiatives and expressions that resonate with the country's rich cultural and spiritual heritage.

The Role of Imagination and Play in Learning

Rudolf Steiner's profound insights on education highlight the recognition of the unique individuality of each child. According to Steiner, every child comes into the world with their own distinct qualities, potential, and destiny. Understanding and nurturing this individuality is at the heart of Waldorf Education.

Steiner emphasizes that children are not blank slates to be filled with information but are, instead, spiritual beings with their own soul qualities and life purpose. As educators, parents, and caregivers, it is crucial to observe and honor each child's individual temperament, talents, and needs. By doing so, we create a learning environment that caters to their distinct development and fosters a sense of self-worth and confidence.

In Waldorf Education, the curriculum is designed to resonate with the developmental stages of the child. Teachers carefully consider the child's age, interests, and capacities when planning lessons and activities. The approach aims to meet children where they are in their unique developmental journey, allowing them to learn and grow at their own pace.

Steiner also emphasizes the importance of allowing children to express themselves creatively. Artistic activities, such as painting, drawing, music, and movement, are integral to the Waldorf curriculum. These activities not only foster creativity and imagination but also provide children with various avenues to explore and communicate their feelings and ideas.

Furthermore, the role of the teacher is that of a guide and facilitator, rather than an authoritarian figure. Teachers seek to build strong relationships with their students, fostering an environment of trust and open communication. Through this supportive connection, teachers can better understand and respond to the needs and individuality of each child.

Rudolf Steiner's teachings emphasize that every child is a unique individual with their own inherent gifts and qualities. Waldorf Education strives to create an environment that respects and nourishes this individuality, allowing each child to unfold and thrive in their own special way. By recognizing and celebrating the uniqueness of each child, we empower them to become confident, self-directed learners, capable of embracing their life's journey with purpose and fulfillment.

In Waldorf Education, the recognition and celebration of the unique individuality of each child are evident in various aspects of the curriculum and teaching methods. Some examples of how Waldorf Education honors the individuality of each child:

- **Multifaceted Learning:** The curriculum in Waldorf schools is designed to cater to different learning styles and interests. Teachers use a variety of teaching methods, including storytelling, artistic activities, movement, and hands-on experiences, to engage children with diverse talents and abilities.

- **Personalized Approach:** Waldorf teachers take the time to get to know each child individually, understanding their strengths, challenges, and learning preferences. This personalized approach allows teachers to tailor their lessons to meet the specific needs of each student.

- **Child-Centered Learning:** In Waldorf classrooms, the focus is on the child as an active participant in the learning process.

Rather than a one-size-fits-all approach, the teacher adapts the lessons to align with the children's developmental stage and interests, fostering a deep and meaningful connection to the subject matter.

- **Arts Integration:** Artistic activities, such as painting, drawing, drama, and music, play a central role in the curriculum. These activities provide children with various means of self-expression and allow them to engage with the subject matter in a creative and individualized way.

- **Encouragement of Self-Discovery:** Waldorf education encourages children to explore their own unique interests and passions. Students are encouraged to engage in self-directed learning and pursue projects that align with their individual inclinations, fostering a sense of autonomy and self-discovery.

- **Flexible Timelines:** Waldorf schools recognize that children develop at their own pace. The flexible approach to learning allows students to progress through the curriculum at a pace that suits their individual needs, providing the opportunity for both academic and emotional growth.

- **Emotional and Social Development:** Waldorf education places a strong emphasis on emotional intelligence and social skills. Teachers work to create a supportive and nurturing environment where children feel safe to express themselves authentically and develop healthy relationships with peers and adults.

- **Individual Milestones:** Teachers celebrate the unique milestones achieved by each child, acknowledging their progress and growth in various aspects of their development.

Waldorf Education seeks to cultivate the whole child, recognizing that each individual brings their own special gifts, challenges, and potentials. By honoring the unique individuality of each child, Waldorf schools create a learning environment that fosters confidence, creativity, and a deep sense of belonging, allowing children to thrive and become well-rounded individuals capable of embracing their life's journey with joy and purpose.

The Importance of Holistic Development

Rudolf Steiner's concept of holistic development is a central principle in Waldorf Education. He believed that true education should not only focus on intellectual learning but should also nurture all aspects of a child's being - body, soul, and spirit. The key elements of holistic development as per Rudolf Steiner:

- **Physical Development:** Steiner emphasized the importance of providing a healthy and nourishing physical environment for children. This includes proper nutrition, ample outdoor play, and a balanced daily routine. Physical activities and movement, such as eurythmy and games, are integrated into the curriculum to promote physical coordination and well-being.

- **Emotional Development:** Waldorf Education recognizes the significance of emotional intelligence in a child's growth. Teachers create a safe and supportive space where children can express their feelings and emotions openly. Storytelling and artistic activities help children connect with their emotions and develop empathy towards others.

- **Intellectual Development:** While holistic development extends beyond intellectual learning, Steiner acknowledged the importance of cultivating thinking capacities. Waldorf education seeks to foster critical thinking, problem-solving skills, and a love for learning. However, this intellectual development is always integrated with artistic and creative activities to provide a well-rounded education.

- **Social Development:** Steiner emphasized the importance of building a strong sense of community within the classroom and school. Children are encouraged to work together, collaborate, and support one another. Social skills, such as communication, cooperation, and conflict resolution, are actively cultivated through group activities and projects.

- **Spiritual Development:** Waldorf Education acknowledges the spiritual dimension of human life, and the curriculum is designed to awaken the child's spiritual potential. While it is not tied to any specific religious dogma, Waldorf education seeks to nurture a child's sense of wonder, reverence for nature, and connection to the world around them.

- **Artistic and Creative Development:** Steiner believed that artistic activities are vital for a child's development. The arts, including painting, drawing, music, drama, and handwork, are integrated into the curriculum at all levels. These activities not only foster creativity but also enhance cognitive abilities and emotional expression.

- **Individuality:** Steiner recognized the uniqueness of each child and the importance of honoring their individuality. Waldorf teachers strive to create a learning environment that allows each child to flourish and reach their full potential in their own unique way.

By embracing these elements of holistic development, Waldorf Education aims to nurture well-rounded individuals who are intellectually capable, emotionally resilient, socially adept, and spiritually aware. The holistic approach fosters a deep love for learning and a lifelong curiosity about the world, preparing children to lead meaningful and fulfilling lives.

The Core Essence of Waldorf Education

The Septennials

The term "septennials" is derived from the Latin word "septennium," which means a period of seven years. It is used to refer to the concept of seven-year cycles in human development. The idea of septennials has its roots in ancient and traditional belief systems that recognized the significance of cycles and rhythms in nature and human life.

The concept of septennials became more prominent and well-defined through the work of Rudolf Steiner, the founder of Anthroposophy and Waldorf education. Steiner introduced the idea of septennials as distinct developmental stages in human life, occurring approximately every seven years. He discussed these stages in the context of spiritual-scientific insights into child development, human biographies, and the spiritual evolution of individuals.

Steiner's lectures and writings on education and human development, including "The Foundations of Human Experience," provided deeper insights into the concept of septennials and how they relate to various aspects of a person's life journey. The term "septennials" became widely used within the context of Waldorf education and other anthroposophically inspired fields, where it has had a significant influence on understanding and supporting the natural rhythms and cycles in human growth and learning.

The word "septennials" emerged from a combination of ancient beliefs about cycles in nature and Steiner's spiritual-scientific explorations of human development, leading to its adoption and application in the context of Anthroposophy and Waldorf education.

Rudolf Steiner spoke about septennials, also known as seven-year cycles, in the context of human development, particularly in his lectures on education and human biographies. He discussed the concept of septennials as part of his broader spiritual-scientific worldview called Anthroposophy.

Steiner's exploration of septennials can be found in various lectures and writings throughout his life, but one of the most well-known works where he discusses this concept is "The Foundations of Human Experience" (also known as "The Study of Man" or "Practical Advice to Teachers"). In this series of lectures, which were delivered to the first Waldorf school teachers in 1919, Steiner outlined his educational philosophy and provided insights into child development.

In these lectures, Steiner introduced the idea of septennials as distinct developmental stages that occur approximately every seven years in a person's life. He emphasized that each septennial brings unique challenges and opportunities for inner growth, and that understanding these stages is crucial for educators to meet the needs of their students effectively.

Apart from "The Foundations of Human Experience," Steiner also addressed the concept of septennials in other lectures and writings related to human development, spiritual science, and education. His discussions on this topic have been widely studied and integrated into the principles and practices of Waldorf education.

It is important to note that while the concept of septennials has been influential in Waldorf education and other anthroposophically inspired fields, it is one aspect of Steiner's broader spiritual-scientific worldview. Steiner's insights on septennials are just one part of his holistic approach to understanding human nature, development, and potential.

Steiner observed that human beings experience significant changes and transformations at these intervals, and he believed that these stages held particular significance for their physical, emotional, and spiritual growth.

The concept of septennials can be traced back to Steiner's spiritual insights and his understanding of the human being as a spiritual being having a physical experience. According to Steiner, each septennial brings unique challenges and opportunities for inner development.

The septennial stages are as follows:

Septennial Cycle	Age Range	Key Characteristics
Early Childhood	0-7 years	Connection to spiritual origins, growth, sensory development, strong family bond. From Oneness with Mother to Growing Autonomy
Middle Childhood	7-14 years	Imagination, creativity, curiosity, early logical thinking. A Fight for, and Commitment To, Life
Adolescence	14-21 years	Self-identity, independence, self-discovery, critical thinking. Wild Emotions, Raging Hormones, Sexuality
Early Adulthood	21-28 years	Higher education, career exploration, spiritual awakening. Play That Turns Toward Responsibility
Adulthood	28-35 years	Personal and professional growth, life choices. The Body In Full Bloom
Midlife	35-42 years	Deepening inner life, self-reflection, midlife considerations. Crisis and Questioning
Spiritual Transformation	42-49 years	Spiritual reflection and transformation. Soul Searching and Wonder
Progressive Insight	49 -56 years	An Ever Growing Vision and Understanding of Life
The Divergence Point	56 -63 years	The Crossroads: Mastery or Revaluation.
Golden Harvest Years	63- 70 years	A Time of Harvesting and Spreading the Wealth, Blessing, grace & opportunity
Life Reflection	7O- Beyond	Take stock of your life, reflecting on the past

The concept of septennials in Waldorf education has practical implications for curriculum development, teaching methods, and understanding the needs of students at different stages of development. By recognizing and honoring the significance of these developmental stages, Waldorf educators can create learning environments that support the unfolding potential of each child and foster their overall well-being.

The concept of septennials proposes that human development occurs in distinct stages or cycles, approximately every seven years. These stages are thought to repeat throughout a person's life, each characterized by specific developmental tasks and opportunities for growth.

The Four-Fold Human Being

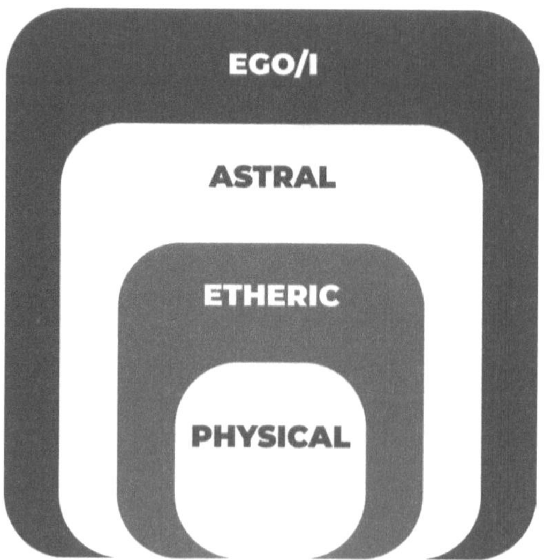

The concept of the fourfold human being is an integral part of Rudolf Steiner's anthroposophical philosophy. It provides a comprehensive understanding of the different aspects that make up the human being and their interconnectedness. Following is a more detailed explanation of the fourfold human being:

Physical Body (Physical Aspect):

The physical body is the visible, tangible aspect of the human being. It is the physical form that interacts with the material world and allows us to perceive the external environment through our senses. The physical body is subject to birth, growth, aging, and eventual death. It is nourished through food and drink and serves as the foundation for our earthly existence.

Etheric Body (Life Aspect):

The etheric body is often referred to as the "life body" or "vital body." It is the dynamic and vital force that animates the physical body and sustains its life processes. The etheric body is responsible for growth, healing, and the regeneration of the physical organism. It forms the template for the physical body's development and plays a crucial role in our overall well-being.

Astral Body (Soul Aspect):

The astral body encompasses the realm of emotions, desires, and sensations. It is associated with our feelings, emotions, passions, and desires. The astral body enables us to experience pleasure, pain, joy, and sorrow. It is the source of our inner life, individuality, and personality. The astral body is also connected to our capacity for imagination, creativity, and artistic expression.

Ego (Individuality Aspect):

The ego, also known as the "I" or individuality, is the core and unique aspect of each human being. It is the center of consciousness and self-awareness. The ego allows us to experience ourselves as distinct individuals with our own thoughts, beliefs, and free will. It provides the capacity for self-reflection, self-determination, and moral responsibility. The development of the ego is seen as a lifelong process, and it plays a crucial role in our spiritual evolution.

According to Steiner, the fourfold human being is not separate entities but interconnected aspects of our individuality. The physical body serves as the vessel for the etheric, astral, and ego aspects to manifest and interact with the material world. The fourfold human being provides a framework for understanding the complexities of human nature, as well as the interplay between the physical, life, soul, and individual aspects.

Steiner's concept of the fourfold human being is an essential foundation in various aspects of anthroposophical philosophy, including education, medicine, and spiritual development. It helps individuals gain a deeper understanding of themselves and their place in the world, fostering personal growth, self-awareness, and a sense of purpose in life.

Human Being Component	Age Range	Characteristics and Developmental Focus
Physical Body	0-7 years	Sensory experiences, motor skill development, and early childhood development.
Etheric or Life Body	7-14 years	Growth, life forces, strengthening the connection between the physical and spiritual worlds. Focus on imagination and creativity.
Astral or Feeling Body	14-21 years	Awakening of emotions, desires, and individuality during adolescence. Learning through inspiration and idealism.
Ego or "I"	21+ years	Full development of individuality, self-awareness, and consciousness in adulthood. Learning through intuition and self-discovery.

Four Elements- Spiritual-scientific worldview

The 4 Elements

As per Rudolf Steiner's spiritual-scientific worldview, the elements of Earth, Water, Air, and Fire hold both physical and spiritual significance. These elements are not merely material substances but are also considered to be manifestations of spiritual forces that underlie the physical world. Steiner described the four elements as follows:-

- **Earth:** The element of Earth represents the solid and substantial aspect of the physical world. It is associated with stability, materiality, and the forces of gravity. In a spiritual context, Earth is related to the realm of the physical body and its connection to the earthly plane. Steiner viewed Earth as a vessel for spiritual forces, providing the foundation for the other elements to manifest.

- **Water:** The element of Water embodies the fluid and dynamic aspect of the physical world. It is associated with the forces of cohesion, adaptability, and change. In a spiritual sense, Water is connected to the realm of emotions and feelings. Steiner saw Water as a medium for the interplay of spiritual forces, allowing for transformation and growth.

- **Air:** The element of Air represents the gaseous and expansive aspect of the physical world. It is associated with the forces of movement, communication, and lightness. In a spiritual context, Air is related to the realm of thought and intellect. Steiner viewed Air as a carrier of spiritual forces, enabling the exchange of ideas and insights.

- **Fire:** The element of Fire embodies the transformative and illuminating aspect of the physical world. It is associated with the forces of warmth, inspiration, and will. In a spiritual sense, Fire is connected to the realm of the spirit and consciousness. Steiner saw Fire as the expression of spiritual forces, providing energy and purpose to the other elements.

Element	Qualities	Spiritual Significance
Earth	Solid, stable, foundational	Associated with the physical and material aspects
Water	Fluid, adaptable, life-giving	Symbolizes the realm of feelings, emotions
Air	Gaseous, expansive, intellectual	Represents thought, ideas, and communication
Fire	Transformative, illuminating	Signifies spirituality, will, and life forces

According to Steiner, these four elements are not separate entities but are interrelated and interconnected, forming the basis of the physical world. They are also considered to be expressions of spiritual forces that work behind the scenes to shape and maintain the material world. Steiner's understanding of the four elements is part of his broader spiritual philosophy, which seeks to explore the relationship between the physical and spiritual dimensions of reality.

The Four Distinct Temperaments:

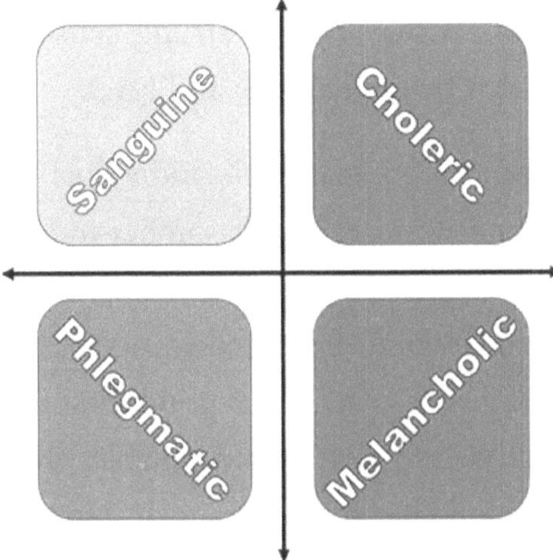

The temperaments alone make all multiplicity, beauty and fullness of life possible - Rudolf Steiner.

The concept of temperaments is a fundamental aspect of his anthroposophical philosophy. According to Steiner, human beings exhibit four distinct temperaments, each characterized by specific personality traits, behavioural tendencies, and ways of experiencing the world. These temperaments are influenced by the interplay of the physical body, etheric body, astral body, and ego within the individual. The four temperaments are:

The Melancholic Temperament:

The melancholic temperament is associated with the earth element and is characterized by introversion, sensitivity, and introspection. Individuals with a melancholic temperament are often deep thinkers, prone to introspection and self-analysis. They can be sensitive to their own emotions and the emotions of others, making them empathetic and compassionate. However, they may also be prone to mood swings and can be introspective to the point of being self-absorbed. Melancholic individuals may have a strong sense of responsibility and duty, and they can be dependable and loyal.

Example: Swapnali is a melancholic individual. She is introverted and often spends time alone, reflecting on her thoughts and feelings. Swapnali is sensitive and empathetic, always understanding and supporting her friends when they need someone to talk to. She can be deeply analytical and is often seen pondering about life's deeper questions. Swapnali is responsible and reliable, always fulfilling her commitments and taking her duties seriously. However, she may also be prone to mood swings and can sometimes be overly critical of herself and others.

The Choleric Temperament:

The choleric temperament is associated with the fire element and is characterized by extroversion, assertiveness, and high energy levels. Choleric individuals are often strong-willed, determined, and goal oriented. They are natural leaders and can be assertive and decisive in their actions. Choleric individuals are driven by a desire for achievement and success and may be competitive and ambitious. However, they may also be prone to impatience and can sometimes be seen as domineering or aggressive.

Example: Johnathan is a choleric individual. He is highly assertive and confident, always taking the lead in group projects and motivating his peers to perform their best. Johnathan is ambitious and driven, setting clear goals for himself and working hard to achieve them. He can be competitive and enjoys challenges that push him to excel.

Johnathan is also impatient at times and may become frustrated if things don't go as planned. However, he is a natural leader and often takes charge in difficult situations.

The Sanguine Temperament:

The sanguine temperament is associated with the air element and is characterized by sociability, enthusiasm, and optimism. Sanguine individuals are often outgoing, talkative, and enjoy being in social settings. They have a natural charm and can easily make friends. Sanguine individuals are typically optimistic and have a positive outlook on life. They are adaptable and flexible, making it easy for them to adjust to new situations and experiences. However, they may be prone to restlessness and may have difficulty focusing on tasks for extended periods.

Example: Sara is a sanguine individual. She is outgoing and friendly, always making new friends and being the life of the party. Sara is enthusiastic and optimistic, seeing the bright side of every situation. She is talkative and enjoys sharing stories and experiences with others. Sara is flexible and adaptable, always open to new ideas and experiences. However, she can also be restless and may have difficulty staying focused on tasks for long periods of time.

The Phlegmatic Temperament:

The phlegmatic temperament is associated with the water element and is characterized by calmness, patience, and a steady temperament. Phlegmatic individuals are often easy-going and laid-back. They are good listeners and can be empathetic and understanding. Phlegmatic individuals are usually reliable and steady, making them good team players. However, they may also be prone to complacency and may have difficulty expressing their emotions.

It is important to note that individuals may exhibit a combination of these temperaments, with one or two temperaments being more dominant than the others. Steiner's understanding of temperaments is not meant to categorize or label individuals but rather to provide insights into the unique personality traits and tendencies that can influence how people relate to themselves and the world around them.

Example: Manish is a phlegmatic individual. He is calm and composed, rarely getting worked up or stressed about things. Manish is patient and understanding, always willing to listen to others and provide a supportive shoulder. He is reliable and consistent, never rushing into decisions but taking his time to weigh the options.

Manish is easy-going and rarely lets things bother him. However, he may also be prone to complacency and may need encouragement to step out of his comfort zone.

It is essential to remember that individuals can have a combination of temperaments, and their behavior and personality can be influenced by various factors such as upbringing, life experiences, and personal growth. The concept of temperaments in Waldorf education helps teachers understand and support each student's unique needs and preferences, creating a harmonious and inclusive learning environment.

Temperament	Characteristics	Elemental Association	Developmental Focus
Melancholic	Introspective, analytical, sensitive, and thoughtful.	Earth	Deepening self-awareness and grounding in practical life.
Sanguine	Enthusiastic, optimistic, social, and expressive.	Air	Nurturing social relationships, empathy, and communication.
Choleric	Assertive, ambitious, independent, and goal-oriented.	Fire	Building self-confidence, inner drive, and self-discipline.
Phlegmatic	Calm, even-tempered, patient, and empathetic.	Water	Cultivating emotional stability, patience, and harmonious relationships.

Bodily fluid theory of temperaments

The bodily fluid theory of temperaments, is based on the ancient concept of the four humors, which dates back to ancient Greek and Roman medicine. According to this theory, the human body is composed of four primary bodily fluids or humors, and an individual's temperament and personality are influenced by the predominance of one or more of these humors. Steiner adapted this ancient theory to his spiritual and anthroposophical worldview, associating each temperament with specific bodily fluids. Steiner's bodily fluid theory of temperaments:

Black Bile (Melancholic):

In Steiner's theory, the Melancholic temperament is associated with black bile, one of the four primary bodily fluids. Black bile was thought to be secreted by the spleen, and its predominance in a person's constitution was believed to lead to a Melancholic temperament. Individuals with this temperament were considered to be introverted, thoughtful, analytical, and emotionally sensitive. They may be prone to mood swings and melancholy.

Phlegm (Phlegmatic):

The Phlegmatic temperament, according to Steiner, is associated with the bodily fluid called phlegm. Phlegm was thought to be produced by the respiratory system, and its prevalence in a person's constitution was believed to result in a Phlegmatic temperament. Individuals with this temperament were considered to be calm, composed, easy-going, patient, and relaxed. They tend to remain unperturbed by external events.

Blood (Sanguine):

Steiner associated the Sanguine temperament with the bodily fluid blood. In ancient humoral theory, blood was believed to be produced by the liver, and its predominance was associated with a Sanguine temperament. Individuals with this temperament were considered to be sociable, outgoing, enthusiastic, expressive, creative, and optimistic. They tend to adapt easily to new situations.

Yellow Bile (Choleric):

The Choleric temperament, according to Steiner, is linked to the bodily fluid called yellow bile. Yellow bile was thought to be secreted by the gallbladder, and its prevalence in a person's constitution was believed to lead to a Choleric temperament. Individuals with this temperament were considered to be energetic, active, assertive, decisive, ambitious, and self-confident. They were seen as natural leaders with strong personalities.

Bodily Fluid	Associated Temperament	Typical Traits
Blood	Sanguine	Cheerful, optimistic, sociable, enthusiastic, outgoing
Phlegm	Phlegmatic	Calm, easygoing, patient, steady, reliable
Yellow Bile	Choleric	Passionate, energetic, assertive, goal-oriented
Black Bile	Melancholic	Introspective, serious, analytical, deep thinker

It is essential to recognize that Steiner's bodily fluid theory of temperaments is rooted in historical and philosophical traditions and may not align with modern scientific understandings of personality and temperament. While this theory may offer valuable insights into Steiner's anthroposophical perspectives on human nature, it should be approached with an appreciation for its historical context and not interpreted as a definitive scientific explanation of human behavior.

4 Kingdoms defined by Rudolf Steiner

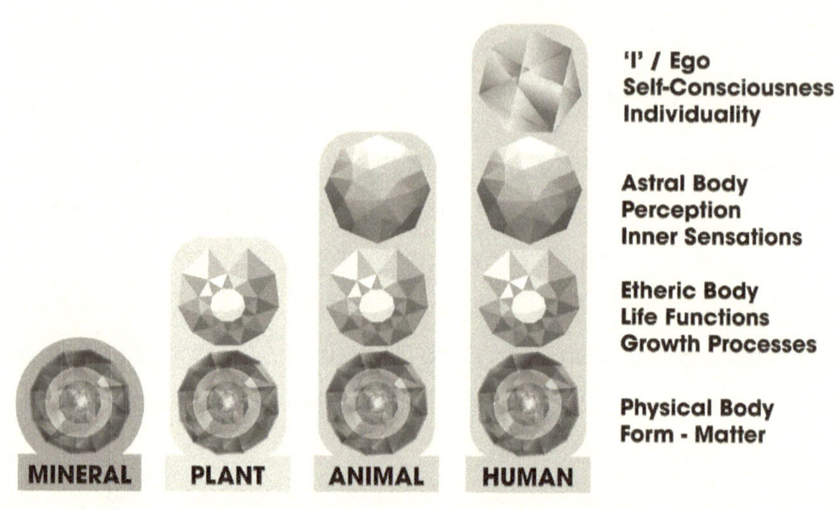

Steiner introduced the concept of the four kingdoms in his spiritual philosophy, Anthroposophy. These four kingdoms represent different realms of existence and consciousness. They are:

Mineral Kingdom:

The mineral kingdom represents the lowest level of consciousness in Steiner's classification. It includes all inanimate matter, such as rocks, minerals, and crystals. According to Steiner, these entities have a very basic form of consciousness, and their existence is primarily physical and fixed. They do not have a life force or capacity for growth and development like living beings.

Plant Kingdom:

The plant kingdom represents the next level of consciousness. Plants are living beings that exhibit characteristics of growth, reproduction, and response to stimuli. Steiner believed that plants possess a life force or etheric body, which enables them to grow, adapt, and interact with their environment. Plants play a vital role in the ecosystem, providing food, shelter, and oxygen for other living beings.

Animal Kingdom:

The animal kingdom represents a higher level of consciousness compared to plants. Animals have a more developed soul life, which includes emotions, instincts, and sensory experiences. They can move, perceive their surroundings, and exhibit behaviors that indicate some level of individuality. Unlike plants, animals possess an astral body, which allows for a more dynamic and responsive experience of the world.

Human Kingdom:

The human kingdom represents the highest level of consciousness according to Steiner's classification. Humans are unique in their capacity for self-awareness, rational thinking, and moral decision-making. They possess a physical body, an etheric body, and an astral body, but what sets them apart is the presence of an individualized, spiritual component known as the ego or "I." This ego gives humans the ability to have a sense of self, freedom of choice, and the potential for spiritual growth.

Steiner's concept of the four kingdoms provides a framework for understanding the diverse forms of existence in the world and the different levels of consciousness associated with them. It also emphasizes the interconnectedness of all living beings and their role in the cosmic order. In Waldorf education, teachers often incorporate these concepts into the curriculum, helping students develop a deeper appreciation for the natural world and their place within it.

Kingdom	Characteristics	Significance
Mineral Kingdom	• Inanimate matter like rocks and minerals	• Forms the physical foundation of the world
Plant Kingdom	• Living plants with growth and form	• Bridge between the physical and spiritual realms
Animal Kingdom	• Mobile, possess instincts, basic consciousness	• Connects the spiritual and physical worlds
Human Kingdom	• Self-aware, moral reasoning, free thinking	• Plays a central role in Earth's spiritual evolution

Bodily System

Rudolf Steiner's teachings regarding the physical, glandular, nervous system, and blood circulation are based on his understanding of the human being's complex constitution. He viewed the human being as a multidimensional entity, consisting of interconnected physical and spiritual aspects. Steiner's insights on these bodily systems are part of his broader anthroposophical understanding of human nature and development.

Physical Body: Steiner acknowledged the importance of the physical body as the instrument through which humans interact with the material world. He emphasized the significance of a healthy and well-balanced physical body for overall well-being and spiritual development. Physical health and vitality are considered essential in Waldorf Education to provide a solid foundation for learning and growth.

Glandular System: Steiner recognized the glandular system's role in regulating various bodily functions and its connection to the subtle spiritual forces at work in the human being. He viewed the glands as not only physical organs but also as centers of spiritual activity that influence the individual's emotional and mental states. The endocrine glands were seen as essential mediators of the soul's activities.

Nervous System: Steiner gave great importance to the nervous system as the physical foundation for human consciousness and cognitive abilities. He believed that the nervous system acts as an intermediary between the physical body and the soul or spirit. Through the nervous system, humans can perceive the external world and process sensory information, which contributes to their inner experiences and understanding.

Blood Circulation: Steiner regarded the blood as a carrier of spiritual forces, not just physical elements. He saw the rhythmic flow of blood as intimately connected to the human soul's life and emotions. The heart's rhythmic beating, which drives blood circulation, was considered a reflection of the human being's inner spiritual life.

Steiner's approach to human physiology integrated both the physical and spiritual aspects of the human being. He believed that understanding the interplay between the physical bodily systems and the soul and spirit could lead to a more profound comprehension of human nature and contribute to personal development and well-being.

These insights into the human constitution influenced various fields, including education, medicine, and spiritual philosophy, and continue to be explored and applied in contemporary anthroposophical practices.

Aspect	Rudolf Steiner's Teachings
Physical Body	• The physical body is the most tangible aspect of an individual. It serves as the instrument for interacting with the physical world. • Steiner believed that the physical world is a reflection of spiritual realities.
Glandular System	• The endocrine system, which includes glands like the pituitary, thyroid, and adrenal glands, is essential for regulating various bodily functions, including growth, metabolism, and emotions. • Steiner emphasized the role of the endocrine system in bridging the physical and spiritual dimensions, influencing overall well-being and development.
Nervous System	• Steiner's teachings go beyond the physical nervous system and encompass the concept of the "etheric body," a non-physical or spiritual aspect of human existence. • The nervous system processes sensory information, thoughts, and emotions and works in harmony with the etheric body to facilitate spiritual experiences and growth.
Blood Circulation	• Steiner had a unique perspective on the circulatory system, viewing the heart as a center for higher spiritual experiences. • He believed the circulatory system plays a crucial role in mediating the relationship between the physical and spiritual aspects of human existence. • A harmonious connection between the circulatory system and the spiritual world is emphasized for overall health and spiritual development.

Rudolf Steiner's theory of the four temperaments encompasses a comprehensive understanding of human nature, incorporating physical, spiritual, and natural elements. Each temperament is associated with a specific aspect of human existence and is influenced by one of the four kingdoms of nature - mineral, plant, animal, and human.

Steiner's Temperament theory & its application:-

Education: Understanding the temperaments and their corresponding bodily systems can help educators tailor their teaching methods to meet the individual needs of students. For example, a melancholic child, associated with the physical aspect and the mineral kingdom, might benefit from structured and analytical learning approaches.

Healthcare: Steiner's temperaments offer insights into an individual's constitution, influencing health and well-being. A person with a phlegmatic temperament, related to the etheric aspect and the plant kingdom, might respond well to natural remedies and holistic healing practices.

Personal Development: Recognizing one's temperament can aid in self-awareness and personal growth. Individuals with a sanguine temperament, connected to the astral aspect and the animal kingdom, might excel in creative pursuits and social interactions.

Examples:

1. A teacher notices that a student who exhibits characteristics of being introverted, thoughtful, and analytical (melancholic temperament) tends to thrive in individual study projects (aligned with the physical aspect) and shows a keen interest in geology (connected to the mineral kingdom).

2. In a healthcare setting, a practitioner takes into account a patient's calm, adaptable, and patient demeanor (phlegmatic temperament) and prescribes herbal remedies (reflecting the plant kingdom) to support their overall well-being.

3. During a team-building exercise, a facilitator observes a participant's sociable, enthusiastic, and creative nature (sanguine temperament) and encourages them to take a leadership role (related to the animal kingdom) in the group.

4. An individual, known for their energetic, assertive, and ambitious qualities (choleric temperament), excels in competitive sports (aligned with the ego aspect) and pursues a career in physical fitness (connected to the physical body).

By understanding and applying the insights from Steiner's theory of the four temperaments, individuals can better navigate their personal and professional lives, leading to a more balanced and harmonious existence in alignment with the rhythms of nature and the human spirit.

12 Senses as per Rudolf Steiner

Rudolf Steiner introduced the concept of 12 senses, they are:

Sr. No	Sense	Related to	Function
1	Touch	Physical	Sensation of pressure, warmth, cold, and texture
2	Life (or Vitality)	Etheric	Awareness of life processes and vitality
3	Movement		Perception of one's own movement and balance
4	Balance		Perception of body orientation in space
5	Smell	Astral	Sensation of different odors and scents
6	Taste		Perception of different tastes and flavors
7	Sight		Visual perception of shapes, colors, and forms
8	Warmth		Sensation of warmth and temperature
9	Hearing		Auditory perception of sounds and noises
10	Speech (or Word/Language)	Ego	Perception of spoken language and communication
11	Thought (or Concept)		Ability to form and understand abstract concepts
12	Ego Sense (or Self-awareness)		Awareness of oneself as an individual being

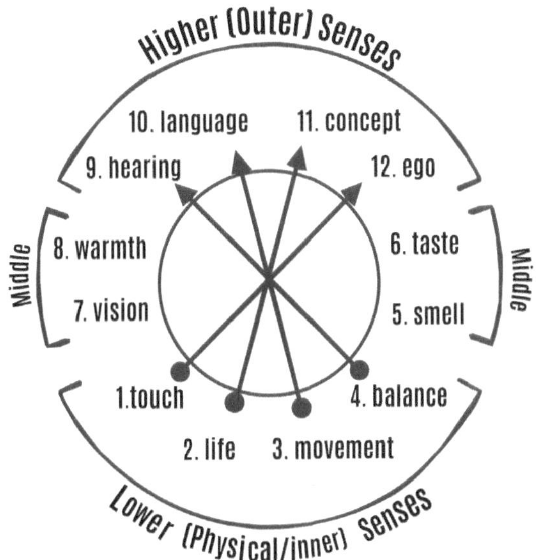

DR. RUDOLF STEINER CONCEPT OF TWELVE SENSES

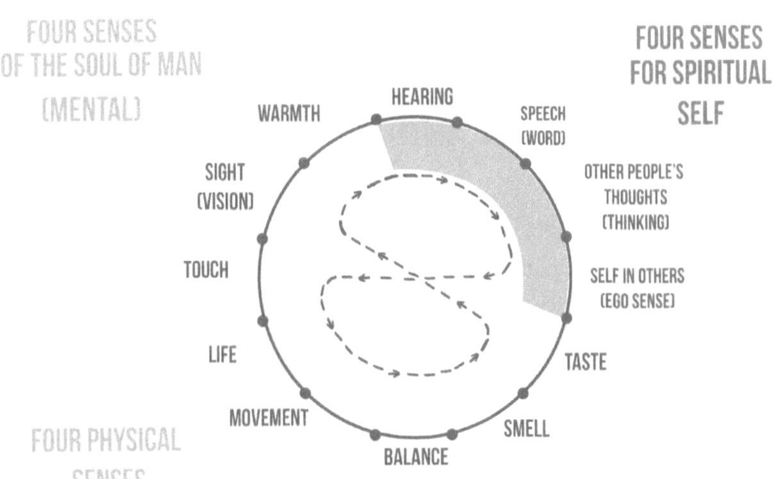

3-Fold Human Being

Rudolf Steiner's concept of the threefold human being is a central aspect of his anthroposophical teachings. According to Steiner, human beings are composed of three distinct but interconnected members: the thinking, feeling, and willing. These three members are not physical entities but rather spiritual aspects that permeate the human being and shape their experience of the world.

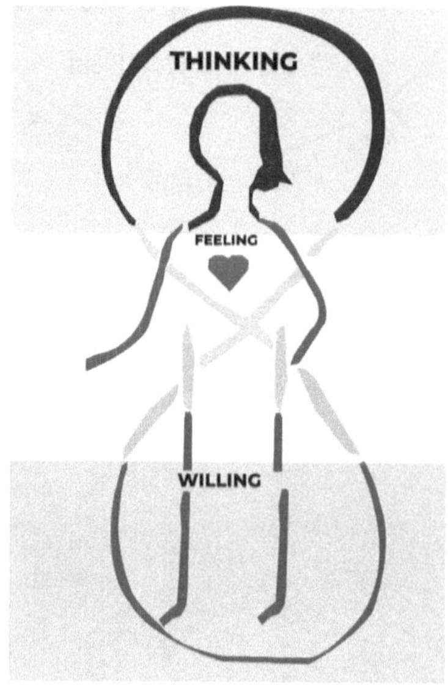

- **Thinking**: The first member of the human being is the thinking, which is associated with the head. It encompasses cognitive processes, logic, reason, and intellectual understanding. Thinking enables us to perceive and comprehend the world around us, to form concepts, and to engage in abstract thought. It is through thinking that we gain knowledge and understanding of the world's laws and principles.

- **Feeling**: The second member is the feeling, which is associated with the heart or chest region. Feeling encompasses emotions, sensations, and the capacity to empathize and connect with others emotionally. Through feeling, we experience the world in a more personal and subjective way, allowing us to form meaningful relationships and experience the full range of human emotions.

- **Willing**: The third member is the willing, which is associated with the limbs and metabolic processes of the human being. Willing is the capacity for action, impulse, and desire. It drives us to engage with the world actively, to make choices, and to carry out our intentions. Willing is closely related to our physical body and our ability to manifest our intentions through physical actions.

Steiner emphasized the importance of maintaining a balance between these three members to achieve holistic human development. He believed that a harmonious interaction among thinking, feeling, and willing is essential for a well-rounded and spiritually developed individual.

The threefold human being also relates to different aspects of human growth and education. In education, Steiner advocated for an approach that addresses the needs of each member separately and fosters their harmonious integration. For example:

In early childhood education, the emphasis is on developing the will through play and hands-on activities that engage the child's physical body.

In middle childhood, the focus shifts to the feeling life, nurturing emotional intelligence and empathy through artistic and social experiences.

In adolescence and beyond, education centers on the cultivation of thinking and intellectual capacities, encouraging critical thinking and independent judgment.

Steiner's concept of the threefold human being provides a holistic framework for understanding human nature and human development. It recognizes the multifaceted nature of the human being and underscores the importance of nurturing all three aspects – thinking, feeling, and willing – to achieve balance and wholeness in life. By cultivating and integrating these three members, individuals can achieve greater self-awareness, spiritual growth, and a more profound connection to the world around them.

The concept of the threefold human being has diverse applications across various fields, including education, healthcare, social organization, and personal development. The Key areas where the threefold human being can be applied are:

- **Education**: In education, the threefold human being serves as a guiding principle for designing a holistic and balanced curriculum. Teachers aim to address the needs of thinking, feeling, and willing in students to support their comprehensive development. This approach recognizes that each aspect requires different methods of teaching and learning to foster a well-rounded education.

- **Healthcare**: In anthroposophical medicine, the threefold human being is used to understand health and illness from a holistic perspective. Practitioners consider the interplay of thinking, feeling, and willing in the human organism and seek to restore balance and harmony between these aspects through personalized treatment plans.

- **Social Organization:** Steiner proposed that society should be organized into three distinct realms: the cultural-spiritual, the economic, and the political. This concept is known as social threefolding. Each realm focuses on specific human aspects, such as education, creativity, and self-development (cultural-spiritual), economic activity and mutual cooperation (economic), and legal and political governance (political). By maintaining the autonomy of each realm while promoting healthy interactions, a more balanced and harmonious society can be achieved.

- **Personal Development:** Individuals can apply the concept of the threefold human being in their own personal growth. Understanding and cultivating thinking, feeling, and willing can lead to self-awareness and self-development. By balancing these aspects, one can achieve inner harmony and a deeper connection with oneself and others.

- **Parenting**: Parents can apply the principles of the threefold human being to raise balanced and emotionally healthy children. Recognizing and nurturing the different aspects in their children helps parents support their overall development and well-being.

- **Interpersonal Relationships:** The concept of the threefold human being can enhance relationships by fostering empathy and understanding. By recognizing the diverse ways in which individuals perceive and experience the world, people can communicate more effectively and build deeper connections.

- **Leadership**: Leaders can apply the threefold human being principles in their leadership styles. By considering the needs of thinking, feeling, and willing in their team members, leaders can create a positive and empowering work environment.

The application of the threefold human being emphasizes the interconnectedness of different aspects of human life. It encourages a holistic approach to various domains, recognizing the importance of balanced development and harmonious relationships for personal and collective well-being. Steiner's vision of the threefold human being provides a profound framework for understanding human nature and promoting the evolution of individuals and society as a whole.

Aspect	Component	Description
Thinking	Head	Relates to cognitive processes, intellect, and logical reasoning. It involves the capacity for analytical thinking and understanding the world through thoughts and concepts.
Feeling	Heart	Refers to emotions, sentiments, and empathic responses. It involves the capacity to experience and express emotions, connect with others, and engage in artistic expression.
Willing	Hand	Pertains to actions, desires, and intentions. It involves the capacity to make decisions, exercise free will, and act upon one's intentions in the world.

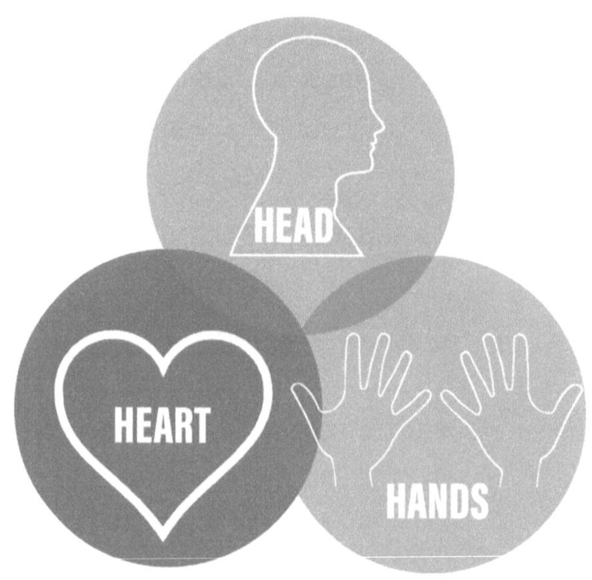

3R's (Rhythm, Reverence, and Repetition)

Rhythm, reverence, and repetition are important principles in Waldorf education, which are based on the insights of Rudolf Steiner. These principles are applied in the classroom and educational practices to create a nurturing and holistic learning environment for students

- **Rhythm:** Rhythm is an essential element in Waldorf education. It refers to the intentional and structured organization of the daily, weekly, and yearly activities in the classroom. Rhythms help create a sense of predictability and stability for the children, which is especially important for their emotional well-being. Daily activities like morning circle time, storytelling, and outdoor play are organized with rhythmic patterns. Weekly and seasonal celebrations, such as festivals and holidays, are also included in the school calendar to provide a rhythmic flow to the year. The regularity and predictability of rhythms help children feel secure and develop a sense of trust in the learning environment.

- **Morning Circle:** Each day begins with a morning circle, where children and teachers gather together. The circle includes singing songs, reciting verses, and engaging in movement exercises to create a harmonious start to the day.

- **Weekly Routines:** Waldorf classrooms have consistent weekly routines that include specific activities on particular days. For example, Mondays may be dedicated to painting, Tuesdays to handwork, and Wednesdays to nature walks. These rhythms provide a sense of structure and anticipation for the children.

- **Seasonal Festivals:** Throughout the year, Waldorf schools celebrate seasonal festivals like Makar Sankranti, Basant Panchami, Pongal, Lohri, Onam & Baisakhi. These festivals mark the changing seasons and foster a connection to nature and the rhythms of the earth.

- **Reverence:** Reverence is the attitude of deep respect, awe, and wonder towards the world and all living beings. In Waldorf education, teachers foster reverence by encouraging a sense of wonder and appreciation for the natural world, the arts, and the human capacity for creativity. Reverence is also nurtured by promoting a sense of gratitude and respect for each other, for cultural diversity, and for the uniqueness of each individual. By cultivating reverence, Waldorf educators aim to inspire a profound connection to the world and a deep sense of responsibility for the well-being of others and the environment.

- **Nature Appreciation:** In Waldorf education, teachers encourage children to observe and appreciate nature. They might take nature walks, create nature tables with found objects from the outdoors, and engage in gardening activities to develop a sense of reverence for the natural world.

- **Respect for Handwork:** Handwork is an important part of the Waldorf curriculum. Children learn to knit, crochet, sew, and work with various materials. They are taught to handle these materials with care and respect, appreciating the effort and skill required to create handcrafted items.

- **Cultural Stories and Tales:** Waldorf teachers share stories and tales from different cultures, fostering an understanding and appreciation for diverse perspectives and traditions.

- **Repetition:** Repetition is a key aspect of learning in Waldorf education. It involves revisiting and reinforcing certain lessons and activities at different stages of a child's development. Through repetition, children have the opportunity to deepen their understanding and internalize concepts more fully. Stories, songs, and verses are often repeated, allowing children to engage with the material at various levels as they grow and develop. Repetition also helps in establishing strong foundations and building skills over time, contributing to a well-rounded and comprehensive education.

- **Morning Verses:** Children often recite morning verses or prayers during the morning circle. These verses are repeated daily, allowing the children to internalize and connect with the words and their meaning.

- **Stories and Fairy Tales:** Many traditional fairy tales and stories are retold several times throughout a child's education in Waldorf schools. Each time the story is revisited, the child gains new insights and deeper understanding as they mature.

- **Main Lesson Blocks:** Waldorf education uses main lesson blocks, where a subject is studied intensively for a period of three to four weeks. The subjects are revisited each year with increasing complexity, reinforcing the learning and building upon previous knowledge.

These principles of rhythm, reverence, and repetition are interwoven into the pedagogical approach of Waldorf education. By incorporating these elements, Waldorf teachers create an enriching and harmonious learning environment that nurtures the child's physical, emotional, intellectual, and spiritual development. These principles are not only limited to classroom practices but also extend to the overall school community and the relationship between teachers, parents, and students.

These principles work together to create a learning environment that is rich in meaning, deeply connected to the world, and supportive of the child's development. Through rhythm, reverence, and repetition, children are guided on a journey of exploration and discovery, cultivating a love for learning and a sense of wonder in their educational experiences.

Creating a Waldorf-Inspired Home Environment

Creating a Waldorf-inspired home involves creating an environment that fosters imagination, creativity, and a sense of connection with nature. The key principles and practical tips to help you create a Waldorf-inspired home:

- **Natural Materials:** Use natural materials in your home decor and furnishings. Choose wooden toys, woollen rugs, cotton or silk fabrics, and natural colors to create a warm and nurturing environment.

- **Rhythms and Routines:** Establish daily, weekly, and seasonal rhythms in your home. This can include having regular meal times, bedtime routines, and celebrating seasonal festivals together as a family.

- **Artistic Expression:** Create opportunities for artistic expression in your home. Set up an art corner with art supplies like colored pencils, beeswax crayons, and watercolors. Encourage your child to engage in free artistic play and storytelling.

- **Storytelling and Books:** Surround your child with age-appropriate books and storytelling. Share fairy tales, folktales, and stories from nature to nourish their imagination and moral understanding.

- **Nature Connection:** Spend time outdoors and bring nature into your home. Display natural treasures like seashells, stones, and pinecones. Consider having plants or a small garden that your child can care for.

- **Free Play and Imaginative Play:** Allow your child plenty of unstructured playtime. Provide simple, open-ended toys like wooden blocks, play silks, and dolls that allow for imaginative play.

- **Screen-Free Environment:** Limit screen time and create a screen-free environment, especially for young children. This encourages them to engage with the real world and foster their creativity.

- **Handwork and Practical Skills:** Introduce handwork and practical skills suitable for your child's age. Let them help with baking, gardening, or knitting to develop their hand-eye coordination and practical abilities.

- **Music and Movement:** Play calming, soothing music in the background and encourage your child to move and dance freely. Sing songs together and consider introducing simple musical instruments.

- **Celebrate Seasons and Festivals:** Embrace the changing seasons and celebrate festivals in a meaningful way. Decorate your home with seasonal crafts, create nature tables, and engage in seasonal activities.

- **Homemade and Natural Toys:** Opt for homemade or natural toys whenever possible. Simple toys made from natural materials can be more enriching and encourage open-ended play.

- **Minimalism and Clutter-Free:** Avoid overwhelming your child with too many toys and clutter. Embrace a minimalist approach to allow them to focus on the simplicity and beauty of their environment.

- **Parent as Guide:** The parent acts as a guide and facilitator rather than an authoritarian. The parent observes the child's interests and needs, providing appropriate learning experiences at home.

Remember that creating a Waldorf-inspired home is about nurturing your child's sense of wonder, fostering creativity, and providing a loving and supportive environment. It's not about adhering to strict rules, but rather about embracing the values and principles that resonate with your family's needs and values. Let your child's interests and developmental stage guide your choices, and enjoy the journey of creating a home filled with warmth, love, and inspiration.

Rhythms, Rituals, and Daily Life

A daily rhythm in a Waldorf-inspired home is designed to provide a sense of predictability, security, and balance for the child.

While each family's rhythm will be unique, here's a sample daily rhythm which we used for Arnav when he was 3 years old and it helped us to create a sense of balance with him.

Morning:

- Wake up and have a cuddle or gentle waking time.

- Engage in a morning verse, song, or a simple gratitude practice.

- Eat a nourishing breakfast together as a family.

- Inclusion in simple morning chores, like making the bed or setting the tables etc.

Late Morning:

- Engage in creative play with open-ended toys like wooden blocks, dolls, or play silks.

- Have a snack with Mother or Grand Mother.

- This is when he was 3 years old and off school

Midday:

- Have a wholesome lunch together with Mother/ Grandmother, emphasizing fresh fruits vegetables & millets bhakri

- Brief period of quiet time or rest time

- Engage in simple handwork or art activities, like drawing, or painting.

Afternoon:

- Enjoy imaginative play and storytelling.

- Participate in a group activity or playdate, like a nature walk in garden or a visit to a local market. Have another snack or tea time with a simple treat.

Evening:

- Help mother with evening chores, like tidying up toys or setting the table for dinner.

- Have a family dinner

- Create a candlelit & cozy atmosphere for sleep

- Wind down with a calming bedtime routine, including a warm bath and a bedtime story.

- Engage in a short bedtime verse or prayer, followed by massage, vibrations & cuddle time before sleep.

It's important to remember that Waldorf-inspired rhythms are flexible and adaptable to the needs of your family and child. You may also include elements like music, movement, and seasonal activities in your daily rhythm. The goal is to create a rhythm that fosters a sense of calm, connection, and joy for both the child and the whole family. As the child grows and changes, the rhythm can be adjusted accordingly to meet their evolving needs and interests.

The Role of the Adult in Early Childhood Education

The role of the adult in early childhood education is of utmost importance. Steiner emphasized that young children are deeply influenced by their environment and the people around them, especially during the first seven years of life. Therefore, the adult's presence, actions, and attitudes play a crucial role in shaping the child's early experiences and development.

The key aspects of the adult's role in early childhood

- **Nurturing and Caring Presence:** The adult, whether it's a parent, teacher, or caregiver, should provide a warm, loving, and nurturing presence for the child. This sense of security and trust is essential for the child's healthy emotional and social development.

- **Modeling Behavior:** Children learn by imitation, and they observe and absorb everything from the adults around them. The adult should strive to model positive behaviors, such as kindness, respect, and empathy, as these qualities will be imprinted upon the child.

- **Creating a Harmonious Environment:** Steiner emphasized the importance of creating a harmonious and aesthetically pleasing environment for young children. The physical surroundings should be simple, orderly, and beautiful, with natural materials and soothing colors.

- **Engaging in Meaningful Activities:** The adult should engage the child in meaningful activities that support their natural curiosity and creativity. This can include simple tasks like cooking, gardening, or artistic activities like painting and handwork.

- **Protecting the Child's Imagination:** Steiner believed that young children have a rich and vivid imagination, and it is essential to protect and nourish this imaginative capacity. The adult should provide opportunities for imaginative play and storytelling.

- **Encouraging Outdoor Play:** Nature holds great significance in Waldorf education, and the adult should encourage ample outdoor play and exploration. Spending time in nature helps children connect with the world and develop a sense of wonder and awe.

- **Creating Rhythms and Rituals:** Steiner emphasized the importance of rhythms and rituals in a child's daily life. The adult should establish consistent daily rhythms and meaningful rituals, like mealtime blessings or bedtime verses, which provide a sense of security and predictability for the child.

- **Observing and Responding:** The adult should be attentive to the child's individual needs and interests. Observing the child closely allows the adult to respond appropriately to their developmental stage and provide the necessary support and guidance.

- **Fostering a Love of Learning:** Early childhood is a time of wonder and exploration. The adult should foster a love of learning in the child by providing a rich and stimulating environment, full of imaginative play, storytelling, and artistic experiences.

Overall, the adult's role in early childhood education is to be a loving and supportive guide, creating a nurturing environment that allows the child to unfold naturally and develop in a healthy and balanced way. Through their thoughtful and intentional interactions, adults can lay the foundation for a lifelong love of learning and a deep connection to the world around them.

Encouraging play and imagination in children

Encouraging play and imagination in children is essential for their healthy development.

Ways to foster play and imagination in line with Steiner's principles:

- **Create an Imaginative Environment:** Provide children with toys and materials that encourage open-ended play and imaginative exploration. Simple, natural toys made from materials like wood, silk, and cotton are often preferred in Waldorf education. These toys allow children to use their imagination to transform them into various objects and characters during play.

- **Limit Screen Time:** Steiner emphasized the importance of limiting screen time, especially for young children. Excessive exposure to screens can hinder imaginative play and interfere with the child's ability to engage with the real world. Instead, encourage children to engage in creative and imaginative play that involves their bodies and senses.

- **Embrace Unstructured Play:** Allow children to engage in unstructured play, where they can freely explore and create without rigid guidelines or adult direction. Unstructured play fosters imagination and allows children to express themselves creatively.

- **Storytelling and Fairy Tales:** Share stories and fairy tales with children. Steiner believed that fairy tales have a deep psychological and spiritual significance for young children. Through storytelling, children can immerse themselves in fantastical worlds and develop a rich inner life.

- **Encourage Outdoor Exploration:** Nature is a rich source of inspiration for the imagination. Encourage outdoor play and exploration, allowing children to connect with the natural world and experience its beauty and wonder.

- **Engage in Dramatic Play:** Set up a dress-up corner or provide props for dramatic play. Children can act out stories and scenarios, giving expression to their thoughts and emotions through role-playing.

- **Foster Artistic Expression:** Provide opportunities for artistic activities like drawing, painting, and modeling with clay. Artistic expression allows children to engage their imagination and create something unique and meaningful.

- **Respect the Child's Inner World:** Acknowledge and respect the child's inner world of imagination and fantasy. Avoid dismissing or trivializing their imaginative play, as it plays a crucial role in their emotional and cognitive development.

- **Rhythms and Rituals:** Establish daily rhythms and rituals that incorporate imaginative elements, such as singing songs, reciting verses, or engaging in finger plays. Rhythms provide a sense of security and predictability for children.

- **Engage in Play Together:** Play with your child and join in their imaginative games. This not only strengthens the parent-child bond but also shows the child that their imaginative play is valued and encouraged.

By creating a nurturing and imaginative environment, limiting screen time, and providing opportunities for unstructured play and artistic expression, parents and educators can support the development of a child's imagination and foster a love for creative exploration.

These practices align with Rudolf Steiner's belief in the importance of play and imagination in a child's early years and contribute to their overall growth and well-being.

Cross the Rainbow Bridge

In Waldorf schools, the concept of "crossing the rainbow bridge" is a symbolic and profound way of addressing transitions and milestones in a child's life, particularly when moving from one grade to another. The idea is inspired by various spiritual and mythological traditions and is woven into the Waldorf educational philosophy.

The "rainbow bridge" represents the journey of a child's growth and development. Each color of the rainbow symbolizes a different stage of a child's life, from early childhood to adolescence. As children progress through these stages, they cross the metaphorical rainbow bridge, signifying their transition from one phase of development to the next.

The rainbow bridge concept acknowledges that children go through distinct and transformative phases, each with its unique qualities and challenges. Waldorf educators emphasize the importance of guiding children through these transitions with care and attention, ensuring that they feel supported and understood during these changes.

Crossing the rainbow bridge is not just a physical transition from one grade to another; it is also an acknowledgment of the child's inner development and the evolving needs of their soul. Waldorf teachers and parents work together to provide an environment that nurtures the child's changing abilities and capacities as they grow.

By using the metaphor of the rainbow bridge, Waldorf schools remind us that education is not just about academic progression but also about recognizing and honoring the emotional and spiritual growth of each child. It underscores the idea that a well-rounded education encompasses not only the acquisition of knowledge but also the development of character and a deep connection with the world.

The significance of crossing the rainbow bridge in Waldorf education lies in its recognition of the child's inner development and the stages of growth that children go through as they progress from early childhood to adolescence. The key aspects of its significance:

1. **Symbol of Transition:** Crossing the rainbow bridge marks the transition from one stage of development to the next. It acknowledges that children's needs and capacities change as they grow, and it provides a symbolic and meaningful way to honor these transitions.

2. **Holistic Growth:** Waldorf education emphasizes holistic development, focusing not only on academic progress but also on the emotional, social, and spiritual aspects of a child's growth. The rainbow bridge signifies this multifaceted development.

3. **Respect for Individuality:** Each child develops at their own pace and in their unique way. The rainbow bridge approach respects the individuality of each child, ensuring that they are supported and guided based on their specific needs and abilities.

4. **Cultural and Mythological Roots:** The concept of the rainbow bridge draws from various cultural and mythological

traditions, adding depth and richness to the educational experience. It connects the child to universal themes of growth and transformation.

5. **Parent-Teacher Collaboration:** Crossing the rainbow bridge involves collaboration between parents and teachers. It fosters a sense of community and shared responsibility for the child's development.

6. **Emotional Support:** Transitioning from one stage to another can be emotionally challenging for children. The rainbow bridge signifies that they are not alone on this journey and that they are supported by a caring and understanding community.

7. **Nurturing the Whole Child:** The significance of the rainbow bridge reinforces the idea that a child's education should be about more than just academic achievement. It should also focus on nurturing qualities like empathy, creativity, and a love for learning.

8. **Spiritual Connection:** Waldorf education places importance on the spiritual dimension of a child's development. Crossing the rainbow bridge can be seen as a spiritual journey, emphasizing the connection between the child's inner world and the world around them.

The significance of crossing the rainbow bridge in Waldorf education is rooted in its holistic and child-centred approach to learning and development. It celebrates the unique journey of each child and the supportive, nurturing community that surrounds them throughout their educational experience.

Rubicon

The ninth year marks a significant turning point in a child's life, akin to crossing a metaphorical Rubicon. It is during this phase that a child begins to detach from their immediate surroundings and starts to distinguish their individual self from the world around them. They establish a sense of autonomy while continuing to hold a deep affection for the environment they are a part of.

In the heart of a quiet suburban Mumbai neighborhood, there lived a mother who found herself on a path less traveled. She was a staunch believer in the principles of Waldorf education, a system that had resonated with her deeply. Her eldest daughter, a sweet and sensitive child, was approaching the age of nine, and as per Waldorf circles, it was a time of crossing the Rubicon. Little did she know that this journey would be one of challenges, triumphs, and profound understanding.

Her nine-year-old daughter, once filled with innocence and wonder, began to show signs of transformation. Anxiety, nightmares, and restless nights became part of their lives. Fears about the unknown, particularly the concept of death, played on the child's mind. The house echoed with door slams, stomping feet, and the occasional rudeness. It was a period of profound change and a sense of separation – what Steiner Waldorf education likened to being thrown out of Paradise. The mother understood the significance of this Rubicon crossing.

As the storms of emotions raged within her daughter, the mother knew that boundaries were crucial. Setting limits on behavior became her unwavering commitment. She navigated the fine balance between strictness and love, providing a safe haven for her child's emotional turmoil. It was a test of patience, as her daughter pushed boundaries to discern whether the adults in her life were truly worthy of respect.

In her quest to understand the changes her daughter was experiencing, the mother asked us for guidance and we turned her to our ultimate resources "Simplicity Parenting" by Kim John Payne. In this resource Payne speaks of prolonged periods of challenging behavior as "Soul Fever." Just as one would care for a child with a physical fever, the child's challenging behavior indicated a deeper struggle. In response, the mother simplified routines, offered more closeness, and listened attentively to her daughter's unspoken fears.

For a while, between the ages of seven and nine, there was a peaceful interlude. Her daughter ventured into the world and brought joy into their lives. However, turning nine in October brought rapid changes. Her child was still a source of joy, but the ebb and flow of emotions was undeniable. This period was like a precursor to adolescence, a glimpse of the future. The mother's heart was filled with mixed feelings as she recognized her child growing away from her.

In her journey through Waldorf-inspired parenting, the mother found solace in the understanding that this Rubicon crossing was part of her child's development. She knew that, as the child matured, things would settle down, and new phases of growth would emerge. She cherished the moments of closeness while navigating the storms of rudeness and rebellion.

The mother's sensitivity to her children's deep feelings compelled her to seek knowledge. Books like "Phases of Childhood" by Bernard C. J. Lievegood provided insights into the complexities of childhood development. She delved into resources focused on the "nine-year change," offering valuable perspectives on Rudolf Steiner's observations.

During this transformative phase, the mother learned not to belittle her child's feelings. The fears, the tears, and the inexplicable worries were real to her daughter. The mother understood the intensity of these emotions and offered solace. She recognized that this wasn't widely understood in the mainstream, and it was a testament to the importance of nurturing children through these developmental transitions.

The Rubicon crossing, as challenging as it was, carried the promise of a smoother adolescence. By understanding and supporting her child during this pivotal stage, the mother hoped to lessen the intensity of future adolescent struggles. She embarked on this journey with faith and patience, knowing that change was the only constant.

In the face of parenting challenges, the mother learned the importance of self-care. She ensured she had enough sleep, a steady routine, and moments for herself. This self-care allowed her to remain grounded, present, and resilient in the face of parenting's peaks and valleys.

Through all the phases of her parenting journey, one phrase remained a constant source of reassurance: "This too shall pass." She learned that parenthood was a voyage marked by ever-shifting tides. Embracing Waldorf-inspired principles, she had faith that all was as it should be, that all was well. Her story was a testament to the profound understanding, growth, and love that arose from crossing the Rubicon in the world of Waldorf education.

The smallest thing in its rightful place can lead to the highest goals.

— Rudolf Steiner

The Waldorf Curriculum and Teaching Methods

We have seen that the Waldorf approach is designed to nurture and support the holistic development of a child, addressing their intellectual, emotional, physical, and spiritual needs.

Principles and aspects of the Waldorf approach to learning:

1. **Holistic Education:** Waldorf education aims to address the whole child, including their intellectual, artistic, practical, and social-emotional development. The curriculum integrates academic subjects with artistic and practical activities to provide a well-rounded education.

2. **Developmental Stages:** The curriculum is tailored to align with the developmental stages of the child. It takes into consideration the specific needs and abilities of children at different ages and focuses on age-appropriate learning activities.

3. **Arts and Creativity:** Artistic activities, such as drawing, painting, music, and handwork, are an integral part of the curriculum. These activities are not only seen as forms of self-expression but also as tools to support cognitive development and learning.

4. **Play and Imagination:** Play is considered an essential element in a child's learning process. Waldorf education encourages imaginative and creative play to foster problem-solving skills and encourage curiosity.

5. **Main Lesson Blocks:** The curriculum is organized into main lesson blocks, which typically last for a few weeks. Each block focuses on a specific subject, allowing students to immerse themselves deeply in the topic.

6. **Limited Use of Technology:** In the early years, Waldorf schools often limit the use of technology, such as computers and screens. Instead, there is an emphasis on direct teacher-student interactions and hands-on learning experiences.

7. **Emphasis on Nature and Outdoors:** Nature is viewed as an important aspect of a child's education. Outdoor activities and nature exploration are incorporated into the learning process.

8. **No Formal Testing:** In the early years, formal testing is generally not used. Instead, teachers assess students' progress through observation, regular evaluations, and ongoing feedback.

9. **Teacher-Student Relationship:** The teacher-student relationship is highly valued in Waldorf education. Teachers often stay with the same group of students for several years, allowing them to develop a deep understanding of each child's individual needs and learning style.

10. **Cultivating Social Responsibility:** Waldorf education aims to foster a sense of social responsibility and respect for others, promoting an inclusive and cooperative classroom environment.

The Waldorf approach to learning seeks to provide a nurturing and enriching educational experience that supports the child's intellectual, emotional, and spiritual growth, helping them to become well-rounded, creative, and compassionate individuals.

The Artistic Approach to Learning

The Artistic Approach to Learning, as per Rudolf Steiner's educational philosophy, is a central element of Waldorf education. It emphasizes the integration of arts and creativity into the learning process to foster holistic development and engage the whole child. The key aspects of the artistic approach to learning:

1. **Arts in the Curriculum:** In Waldorf education, the arts are not considered as separate subjects but are deeply integrated into the curriculum. Drawing, painting, music, drama, and handwork are woven into academic lessons, providing students with multiple ways to engage with the material.

   o Students create paintings or drawings to illustrate stories from history or literature.

   o Music and singing are used to teach mathematical concepts such as rhythm and patterns.

   o Handwork projects, like knitting or sewing, are integrated into lessons to reinforce mathematical skills.

2. **Development of Imagination:** The artistic approach nurtures the child's imagination and creative thinking. Storytelling and imaginative play are used to present academic subjects, allowing students to envision and connect with the content in a vivid and meaningful way.

- Students engage in imaginative play, such as acting out scenes from stories they've heard in class.

- Storytelling sessions are accompanied by vivid descriptions and creative narratives to capture the students' imagination.

The artistic approach nurtures the child's imagination and creative thinking. Storytelling and imaginative play are used to present academic subjects, allowing students to envision and connect with the content in a vivid and meaningful way.

3. **Expressive Arts:** Artistic activities serve as a form of self-expression, allowing students to communicate their thoughts, feelings, and ideas in a non-verbal manner. This can be especially valuable for students who may find it challenging to express themselves verbally.

- Students express their emotions through drawing or painting during art class.

- They may create a visual representation of their feelings after reading a particularly moving poem or story.

4. **Engagement of the Senses:** The arts engage the senses and provide a multi-dimensional learning experience. Whether it's listening to music, working with clay, or performing in a play, students actively participate and learn through their senses.

- Students learn about different cultures through dance, music, and art, allowing them to experience the sights and sounds of various traditions.

5. **Encouragement of Creativity:** Waldorf education places a strong emphasis on fostering creativity. Artistic activities are designed to stimulate the child's imagination and encourage original thinking.

o   During art sessions, students are encouraged to explore their own unique artistic styles and experiment with different materials.

6. **Emotional and Aesthetic Development:** Engaging with the arts can evoke emotional responses and appreciation for beauty. Through exposure to various art forms, students develop an aesthetic sensibility and an understanding of the role of art in human expression.

    o   Students attend live performances, such as theater or music concerts, to experience and appreciate artistic expressions.

7. **Artistic Media and Techniques:** Students are exposed to a variety of artistic media and techniques, enabling them to explore different forms of expression and develop their artistic skills.

    o   In handwork class, students learn different stitching techniques to create practical items like scarves or pouches.

8. **Artistic Practitioners:** Waldorf schools often invite practicing artists and craftsmen to share their expertise with the students. This exposure to professional artists provides inspiration and a deeper understanding of the artistic process.

    o   Visiting artists may teach students about pottery, and they can experiment with shaping clay on the potter's wheel.

9. **Integration with Academic Subjects:** The artistic approach is used to enliven academic subjects such as history, science, and mathematics. For example, students may create paintings, drawings, or models related to historical events or scientific concepts.

    o   In history class, students may create dioramas or models of historical landmarks to deepen their understanding of the time period.

10. **Nurturing Inner Life:** The arts provide an opportunity for inner reflection and contemplation, fostering a rich inner life and a sense of wonder in students.

   ○ During meditation or quiet time, students may create mandalas or draw images that represent their inner thoughts and feelings.

The artistic approach to learning in Waldorf education enriches the learning experience, supports the development of creativity and self-expression, and nurtures the child's emotional, intellectual, and spiritual growth. By engaging the whole child through the arts, Waldorf education seeks to cultivate well-rounded, imaginative, and culturally aware individuals.

The artistic approach is interwoven throughout various subjects and activities in Waldorf education. By embracing the arts and creativity, students can develop a deeper connection to their learning, express themselves more fully, and develop a well-rounded appreciation for beauty and culture.

The Role of Arts, Handwork, and Movement in Education

The role of art in education has a profound impact on students' overall development and learning experiences. What are some of the significant impacts of arts in Education:

1. **Fosters Creativity:** Art encourages students to think creatively and express themselves in unique and original ways. It allows them to explore different ideas, experiment with various materials, and develop innovative solutions to problems.

2. **Enhances Cognitive Development:** Art activities engage various cognitive processes, such as critical thinking, problem-solving, and spatial reasoning. Creating art requires planning, decision-making, and attention to detail, which contribute to cognitive growth.

3. **Improves Motor Skills:** Artistic activities, such as drawing, painting, and sculpting, involve fine motor skills. Regular practice of these activities helps students refine their hand-eye coordination and dexterity.

4. **Boosts Emotional Expression:** Art provides a safe outlet for students to express their emotions and feelings. It can be a therapeutic medium to communicate and process complex emotions that may be challenging to articulate through words.

5. **Encourages Perseverance and Resilience:** Creating art requires patience and perseverance, as it often involves multiple attempts and revisions. Through the artistic process, students learn to embrace mistakes and setbacks, developing resilience and a growth mindset.

6. **Cultivates Cultural Awareness:** Art exposes students to diverse cultures, traditions, and artistic expressions from around the world. This exposure fosters an appreciation for cultural diversity and promotes intercultural understanding.

7. **Supports Academic Learning:** Art can be integrated into various academic subjects, such as history, literature, and science. By incorporating art into the curriculum, students gain a deeper understanding of the subject matter and can make meaningful connections.

8. **Enhances Social Skills:** Collaborative art projects encourage teamwork and cooperation among students. Working together on a shared artistic vision helps students develop communication skills and build positive relationships with their peers.

9. **Promotes Self-Expression and Identity:** Art allows students to explore their identities, interests, and beliefs. It provides a medium for self-discovery and self-expression, fostering a strong sense of self-awareness and confidence.

10. **Inspires Appreciation for Beauty:** Engaging with art, whether through creating it or appreciating others' work, cultivates a sense of beauty and aesthetics. This appreciation extends beyond the art classroom and enhances students' sensitivity to beauty in the world around them.

11. **Reduces Stress and Anxiety:** Art has therapeutic benefits and can serve as a stress-relief outlet for students. Engaging in artistic activities can help reduce anxiety and promote overall well-being.

12. **Builds Cultural Legacy:** Through art, students contribute to their cultural legacy by creating tangible representations of their time and experiences. Their artwork becomes a part of their personal and collective history.

The role of art in education goes beyond just learning artistic techniques. It enriches students' lives, supports their holistic development, and nurtures their creativity and imagination, preparing them to become well-rounded individuals capable of navigating the complexities of the world with wisdom and compassion.

The Role of Movement in education

The role of movement in education has a profound impact on students' learning, development, and overall well-being.

What are some of the significant impacts of incorporating movement into the educational environment:

1. **Enhances Learning:** Movement helps activate multiple areas of the brain, leading to increased cognitive function and enhanced learning. It improves memory retention, attention span, and information processing, making learning more effective.

2. **Supports Brain Development:** Movement activities stimulate the growth of neural connections in the brain, especially in the early years of development. This helps in the formation of a strong foundation for future learning and cognitive abilities.

3. **Increases Engagement:** Active learning through movement makes the learning process more engaging and enjoyable for students. It reduces boredom and monotony, leading to better focus and participation in classroom activities.

4. **Improves Physical Health:** Regular movement activities contribute to improved physical health, including better cardiovascular fitness, muscular strength, and coordination. It also helps in maintaining a healthy body weight and promoting overall well-being.

5. **Reduces Stress and Anxiety:** Movement is known to have stress-relieving effects. Physical activities, such as age appropriate Eurythmy or movement or outdoor play, can help reduce stress and anxiety levels in students, creating a positive and conducive learning environment.

6. **Enhances Social Skills:** Group movement activities encourage collaboration, teamwork, and communication among students. Working together towards a common goal fosters social interactions and strengthens interpersonal skills.

7. **Develops Gross and Fine Motor Skills:** Different types of movement activities, such as running, jumping, drawing, and cutting, promote the development of both gross and fine motor skills in children. These skills are essential for various everyday tasks and academic activities.

8. **Stimulates Imagination and Creativity:** Movement activities often involve imaginative play and storytelling, which sparks creativity and imaginative thinking in children. It allows them to express themselves freely and explore their creativity.

9. **Supports Emotional Regulation:** Movement helps children release pent-up energy and express their emotions in a healthy manner. It can be an effective way to channel emotions and improve emotional regulation.

10. **Cultivates a Healthy Lifestyle:** Introducing movement at an early age fosters a habit of physical activity, promoting a healthy lifestyle throughout life. It encourages students to be active and make healthy choices in their daily lives.

11. **Boosts Academic Performance:** Research has shown that regular physical activity is associated with improved academic performance. Movement breaks during learning sessions can re-energize students and help them better focus on academic tasks.

12. **Fosters a Sense of Freedom and Joy:** Movement allows students to experience a sense of freedom and joy in the learning

process. It creates a positive association with education, making students more enthusiastic about learning.

Incorporating movement into education creates a holistic and dynamic learning environment. It nurtures students' physical, cognitive, social, and emotional development, promoting a well-rounded education that prepares them for success in all aspects of life.

The Role of Handwork in education

Handwork, or handcrafts, holds a special place in the realm of education, and its profound impact is particularly pronounced within the context of the Waldorf approach to holistic learning. In Waldorf education, which emphasizes a balanced and comprehensive development of the child, handwork is not merely a creative outlet but a transformative and integral component of the learning journey.

What are some of the key impacts of handwork in education:

1. **Cognitive Development:** Handwork activities involve problem-solving, pattern recognition, and mathematical thinking. Children learn to follow instructions, plan their work, and use spatial reasoning, which supports cognitive development.

2. **Fine Motor Skills:** Engaging in handwork tasks like knitting, crocheting, or sewing helps develop fine motor skills and hand-eye coordination. These skills are essential for tasks such as writing and drawing.

3. **Focus and Concentration:** Handwork requires sustained attention and concentration. Children learn to focus on their work, leading to improved concentration and attention span in other areas of learning.

4. **Creativity and Imagination:** Handwork encourages creativity and imagination as children have the freedom to design and create their own projects. This fosters a sense of individuality and self-expression.

5. **Emotional Development:** Handwork can be therapeutic and calming, reducing stress and anxiety. Children often find it comforting to engage in repetitive hand movements, which can have a soothing effect.

6. **Sense of Accomplishment:** Completing a handwork project gives children a sense of achievement and boosts their self-esteem. They take pride in their creations and feel a sense of ownership over their work.

7. **Cultural Appreciation:** Handwork often involves traditional crafts that have cultural significance. Children learn about different cultures and appreciate the value of handmade items.

8. **Connection with Nature:** Many handwork materials come from nature, such as wool and wood. This fosters a connection with the natural world and promotes sustainability.

9. **Practical Life Skills:** Handwork teaches practical skills that children can apply in their daily lives, such as sewing on a button or mending a tear.

10. **Social Skills:** Handwork can be done in a group setting, promoting cooperation, teamwork, and social interaction among children.

11. **Integration with Academic Learning:** Handwork can be integrated into academic subjects, reinforcing learning and making abstract concepts more tangible.

12. **Attention to Detail:** Handwork requires careful attention to detail, which enhances observation skills and precision.

In the Waldorf education system, handwork is considered an essential part of the curriculum as it addresses the development of the whole child—head, heart, and hands.

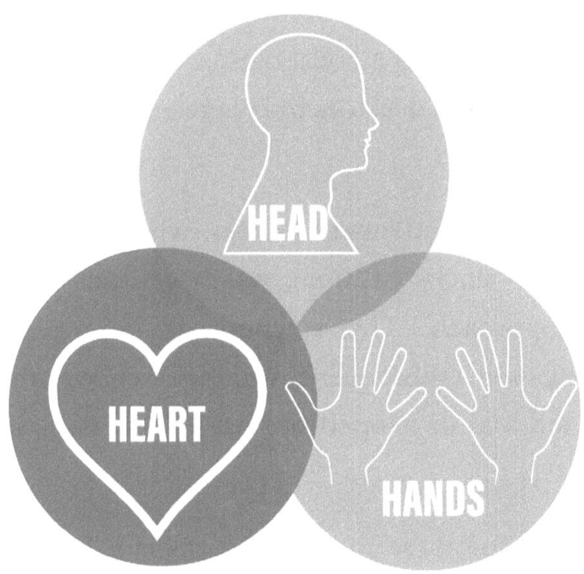

Through handwork, children not only gain practical skills but also engage in activities that nourish their souls, stimulate their minds, and foster a love for learning.

In Waldorf education, these artistic approaches play a vital role in nurturing the child's development and fostering a love for learning. By incorporating artistic activities into the curriculum, educators can create a rich and engaging learning environment that nourishes the child's body, soul, and spirit.

Integrating Academic Subjects through Thematic Blocks

Thematic blocks in Waldorf education were not invented by a single individual. They are a fundamental aspect of the Waldorf pedagogy. Steiner founded the first Waldorf school in Stuttgart, Germany, in 1919.

However, the development of the Waldorf curriculum and pedagogical methods was a collaborative effort involving Steiner, a group of teachers, and educators who were inspired by his educational philosophy.

The idea of using thematic blocks, where subjects are taught in concentrated blocks of time, was a central part of Steiner's educational approach. The teachers at the original Waldorf School, along with subsequent Waldorf schools that followed, further refined and developed the use of thematic blocks in the curriculum.

The purpose of these thematic blocks is to create an in-depth and immersive learning experience for students. Each block typically focuses on one subject or theme, allowing students to explore it deeply and meaningfully before moving on to the next block. This approach is believed to foster a more profound understanding of the subject matter and engage students in a way that supports their cognitive, emotional, and artistic development.

In Waldorf education, thematic blocks are an essential component of the curriculum. Thematic blocks are extended periods of time (usually around 3-4 weeks) during which students focus intensively on a single subject or theme. These blocks allow for in-depth exploration and immersion into a particular topic, providing a more meaningful and comprehensive learning experience.

What are the key aspects of thematic blocks in Waldorf education:

1. **In-Depth Study:** Thematic blocks allow students to delve deeply into a subject, gaining a comprehensive understanding of the topic.

2. **Immersion and Concentration:** By focusing on one subject for an extended period, students can concentrate their attention, promoting a deeper level of engagement and learning.

3. **Integration of Subjects:** Thematic blocks often integrate various subjects such as language arts, science, history, and arts, providing a holistic view of the topic.

4. **Cyclic Approach:** The curriculum in Waldorf education follows a cyclical pattern, revisiting subjects in different grade levels with increasing complexity and depth.

5. **Connection to Child Development:** The choice of themes and subjects in each grade aligns with the developmental stage of the child, addressing their evolving interests and abilities.

6. **Hands-On Learning:** Thematic blocks emphasize experiential and artistic learning, allowing students to engage actively in the subject matter.

7. **Connection to the Seasons and Festivals:** Some thematic blocks are aligned with seasonal changes and cultural festivals, connecting education to the natural and cultural rhythms.

8. **Teacher Creativity:** Waldorf teachers have the flexibility to adapt and tailor the thematic blocks to suit the unique needs and interests of their students.

9. **Storytelling and Imagination:** Storytelling plays a significant role in Waldorf education, weaving together the content of the thematic block and igniting the students' imagination.

Examples of Thematic Blocks in Waldorf Education:

- **Fairy Tales and Legends:** Students explore traditional fairy tales and mythological stories, delving into cultural narratives and moral themes.

- **Ancient Civilizations:** An in-depth study of ancient civilizations, such as India, Egypt, Greece or Rome including historical, cultural, and artistic aspects.

- **Botany and Zoology:** Students learn about plants and animals, their characteristics, life cycles, and ecological roles.

- **Human Anatomy:** An exploration of the human body and its systems, combining biology with artistic activities like drawing and modeling.

- **Mathematics in Nature:** Students explore the mathematical patterns and concepts found in nature, like Fibonacci sequences and geometric shapes.

- **Local Geography and History:** An investigation of the local environment, history, and culture, fostering a sense of connection to the community.

Thematic blocks in Waldorf education provide a rich and varied educational experience, nurturing the child's curiosity, creativity, and love for learning. They also contribute to a balanced and well-rounded development of the child's intellectual, emotional, and physical faculties.

Waldorf schools in India generally follow the same principles of thematic blocks as in other Waldorf schools worldwide. However, it's important to note that individual Waldorf schools adapt the curriculum and thematic blocks to suit the cultural and regional context of India.

In Indian Waldorf schools, thematic blocks are typically organized around various subjects and themes, allowing students to delve deeply into a topic for a concentrated period. The blocks usually last for about 3 to 4 weeks, during which the main lessons revolve around the chosen subject. Some common examples of thematic blocks in Indian Waldorf schools include:

1. **Language Arts:** Thematic blocks for language arts may focus on storytelling, poetry, or exploring specific literary genres. Students engage in various language-related activities, such as creative writing, reading, and recitation.

2. **Mathematics:** Thematic blocks for mathematics often delve into specific mathematical concepts, such as geometry, fractions, or algebra. The lessons are designed to be experiential and hands-on, promoting a deep understanding of mathematical principles.

3. **Science:** Science blocks may cover topics like botany, zoology, physics, or astronomy. Students engage in practical experiments, observations, and nature studies to develop their scientific inquiry skills.

4. **History and Geography:** Thematic blocks in history and geography explore different cultures, historical periods, or geographical regions. Students gain insights into the world's diverse cultures and human history.

5. **Handwork and Arts:** Thematic blocks for handwork and arts may involve working with specific artistic techniques, such as painting, clay modeling, knitting, or woodworking. Students explore their creativity and artistic expression during these blocks.

The impact of thematic blocks on the personality of students in Indian Waldorf schools is similar to that in other Waldorf schools. By focusing on one subject in-depth, students develop a strong connection to the topic and a deeper understanding of the subject matter. Thematic blocks also encourage students to engage in active, experiential learning, which fosters critical thinking, creativity, and a love for learning.

Additionally, these thematic blocks contribute to the holistic development of the child by nurturing their intellectual, emotional, and artistic capacities. The rhythmic and immersive nature of thematic blocks helps create a harmonious and balanced learning environment, supporting the child's growth on multiple levels.

The specific implementation of thematic blocks may vary from one Waldorf school to another, and the curriculum may evolve over time based on the school's unique vision and the needs of the students.

Fostering Creativity and Critical Thinking

Critical thinking is a cognitive process that involves analyzing, evaluating, and synthesizing information to make informed decisions, solve problems, and form well-reasoned judgments. It goes beyond simply accepting or rejecting information at face value and instead involves questioning, reasoning, and examining evidence and arguments to arrive at logical conclusions.

Key aspects of critical thinking include:

1. **Analysis:** Critical thinkers break down complex information into its component parts to understand the underlying structure and relationships between different elements.

2. **Evaluation:** They assess the credibility, validity, and reliability of information, sources, and arguments, considering factors such as evidence, bias, and context.

3. **Inference:** Critical thinkers draw logical inferences and conclusions based on the available evidence and reasoning.

4. **Deduction and Induction:** They use deductive reasoning to reach specific conclusions from general principles, and inductive reasoning to form general principles from specific observations.

5. **Problem-Solving:** Critical thinkers approach problems systematically, considering multiple solutions and evaluating their potential outcomes.

6. **Creativity:** While critical thinking involves analytical skills, it also requires creative thinking to explore innovative and out-of-the-box solutions.

7. **Reflection:** Critical thinkers reflect on their own thought processes, biases, and assumptions, seeking to refine their thinking and develop intellectual humility.

8. **Communication:** They can effectively communicate their ideas and reasoning, supporting their arguments with evidence and clear explanations.

Critical thinking is an essential skill in various areas of life, including education, professional work, decision-making, and problem-solving. It empowers individuals to be more discerning consumers of information, better problem solvers, and more independent and analytical thinkers. In education, promoting critical thinking helps students become active learners, capable of engaging with complex issues and contributing to a deeper understanding of the world around them.

There are several models of critical thinking that have been developed by scholars and educators to provide a structured approach to the process. Some of the most well-known models include:

1. **Paul-Elder Model:** Developed by Richard Paul and Linda Elder, this model emphasizes the elements of critical thinking, including purpose, questions, information, inference, concepts, assumptions, implications, points of view, and context. It encourages thinkers to identify and analyze each of these elements when engaging in critical thinking.

2. **Bloom's Taxonomy:** While not solely focused on critical thinking, Bloom's Taxonomy is a hierarchical model that classifies cognitive processes. It starts with lower-order thinking skills (e.g., remembering and understanding) and progresses to higher-order

thinking skills (e.g., analyzing, evaluating, and creating), which are central to critical thinking.

3. **The RED Model:** Developed by the Foundation for Critical Thinking, the RED Model stands for Recognize assumptions, Evaluate information, Draw conclusions. It provides a simple and practical approach to critical thinking.

4. **The APA Delphi Report:** This model, created by the American Psychological Association, identifies critical thinking as a combination of skills, dispositions, and abilities that involve metacognition, problem-solving, and communication.

5. **The Paulian Framework for Critical Thinking:** Another model by Richard Paul, this framework identifies critical thinking as having four components: the elements of thought, the standards for thinking, the intellectual traits, and the intellectual standards.

6. **The Reasoning Wheel:** Created by Robert Fisher, this model is represented as a wheel with six interconnected aspects of reasoning: analysis, inference, deduction, induction, evaluation, and reflection.

Each of these models provides a structured and systematic way to approach critical thinking, but they all share the common goal of fostering intellectual independence, sound reasoning, and effective problem-solving skills. Educators often incorporate these models into their teaching to help students develop their critical thinking abilities. **Waldorf education fundamentally works on development of critical thinking through it unique interwoven design.**

Critical thinking is often considered a direct indicator of performance in various aspects of life, including academic, professional, and personal domains. How does critical thinking impacts performance:-

1. **Academic Performance:** Critical thinking skills are essential for academic success. Students who can think critically are better able to analyse information, evaluate evidence, and make well-informed decisions. They can apply critical thinking to problem-solving tasks, which leads to better grades and academic achievements.

2. **Professional Performance:** In the workplace, critical thinking is highly valued. Employees who can think critically can identify and solve complex problems, make informed decisions, and innovate. They are more likely to succeed in their roles, adapt to changing circumstances, and contribute to the success of their organization.

3. **Decision Making:** Critical thinking enables individuals to make better decisions. It involves considering multiple perspectives, weighing evidence, and evaluating potential outcomes. Good decision-making skills are crucial in both personal and professional life, as they lead to more favorable and well-thought-out choices.

4. **Problem Solving:** Critical thinking is at the core of effective problem-solving. When faced with challenges, individuals who can think critically are better equipped to analyze the problem, identify potential solutions, and implement the most suitable course of action.

5. **Creativity and Innovation:** Critical thinking is closely connected to creativity and innovation. It allows individuals to explore new ideas, challenge existing assumptions, and generate novel solutions to complex problems.

6. **Communication:** Those who can think critically are more likely to communicate effectively. They can articulate their thoughts, express ideas clearly, and engage in meaningful discussions, leading to improved interpersonal and professional relationships.

7. **Personal Growth:** Critical thinking is not only beneficial for academic and professional success but also for personal growth. It encourages individuals to reflect on their own beliefs and biases, leading to increased self-awareness and personal development.

Critical thinking plays a significant role in determining an individual's performance and success in various aspects of life. It is a skill that can be developed and honed over time through practice and thoughtful engagement with the world around us. Through the beautiful interwoven design Waldorf education naturally develops Critical thinking. It is my personal claim & belief that children who have undergone Waldorf education will score higher in the assessments like Watson Glaser Critical thinking by Pearson which are used in the corporate world for checking critical thinking.

Fostering Creativity through Waldorf Education
Waldorf education is known for its emphasis on fostering creativity in students. Several aspects of the Waldorf approach contribute to driving creativity:

1. **Arts-Integrated Curriculum:** In Waldorf education, the arts are integrated into various subjects, allowing students to engage in creative expression regularly. Drawing, painting, music, drama, and handwork are essential components of the curriculum. Through artistic activities, students develop their imagination, intuition, and creative problem-solving skills.

2. **Play and Imaginative Activities:** Waldorf education recognizes the importance of play in a child's development. Young children are encouraged to engage in imaginative play, which helps them explore their creativity and inventiveness.

3. **Emphasis on Storytelling:** Storytelling is a significant part of Waldorf education. Teachers often use storytelling as a way to present lessons and concepts. This approach stimulates students' imagination, sparking their creativity and curiosity.

4. **Holistic Learning:** Waldorf education considers the whole child, including their emotional, social, and spiritual development, alongside academics. A balanced and holistic approach to education nurtures students' creativity and encourages them to express themselves authentically.

5. **Nurturing Individuality:** Waldorf schools aim to foster each child's unique talents and interests. By recognizing and supporting individuality, students feel empowered to express themselves creatively and pursue their passions.

6. **Focus on Nature and Outdoor Education:** Waldorf education places value on spending time in nature and the outdoors. Outdoor activities inspire a sense of wonder and connection to the natural world, fueling students' creativity and appreciation for the environment.

7. **Limited Use of Technology:** Waldorf schools typically limit the use of technology in the early years of education. This approach allows children to engage with the physical world and encourages hands-on, imaginative play.

8. **Slow Paced Learning:** Waldorf education emphasizes a unhurried and slow-paced approach to learning. This gives students the time and space to explore subjects deeply, make connections, and develop their creative thinking.

9. **Emphasis on Artistic Process:** In Waldorf education, the focus is often placed on the artistic process rather than just the end result. This encourages students to enjoy the creative journey and develop a love for art and self-expression.

By providing a nurturing and imaginative learning environment, Waldorf education stimulates creativity in students and fosters a lifelong love for learning and creative expression.

One can ascend to a higher development only by bringing
rhythm and repetition into one's life. Rhythm holds sway in
all nature.

– Rudolf Steiner

Rhythms and Rituals in Waldorf Education

Rhythms play a crucial role in Waldorf education as they create a harmonious and predictable environment for children to learn and grow. These rhythms can be seen at various levels within the Waldorf educational approach:

1. **Daily Rhythms:** Each day in a Waldorf school follows a predictable rhythm. Activities are structured in a way that allows students to transition smoothly between different subjects and tasks. The day typically starts with a calm and purposeful opening, followed by main lesson blocks in the morning when the children are most attentive. Afternoons often involve artistic activities, outdoor play, and practical work.

2. **Weekly Rhythms:** Waldorf schools often have a seven-day weekly rhythm, with a six-day school week and one day for rest and family activities. The days of the week may be associated with specific activities or themes, such as gardening on certain days, artistic activities on others, or a special assembly or celebration on a particular day of the week.

3. **Seasonal Rhythms:** Waldorf education acknowledges and celebrates the changing seasons. Seasonal festivals and activities are integrated into the curriculum to connect children with nature

and the natural rhythms of the year. For example, students may celebrate the harvest festival, solstices, equinoxes, and other seasonal events.

4. **Main Lesson Blocks:** The main lesson blocks are a significant aspect of the Waldorf curriculum. Each subject is taught in focused blocks of two to four weeks, allowing students to immerse themselves deeply in a topic before moving on to the next. This rhythmic structure aids in concentration, retention, and the integration of knowledge.

5. **Biographical Rhythms:** Waldorf educators are attentive to the developmental stages and needs of each child. They consider the biographical rhythms of a child's life, such as the transition from early childhood to adolescence, and adapt the curriculum and teaching methods accordingly.

6. **Breathing Rhythms:** In the classroom, teachers use breathing rhythms to create a calm and focused atmosphere. Moments of activity are balanced with moments of quiet reflection or contemplation, helping students find balance and concentration.

7. **Teacher Preparation Rhythms:** Waldorf teachers carefully plan and prepare their lessons, following a rhythmic approach that aligns with the developmental needs of their students. This helps teachers maintain their own balance and creativity in the classroom.

These various rhythms in Waldorf education contribute to a sense of security and stability for students. The predictability and regularity of the rhythms help children feel grounded, enabling them to engage more fully in their learning and creative activities. Additionally, the emphasis on nature's rhythms and the interconnectedness of all things fosters a deeper sense of belonging and appreciation for the world around them.

Rhythm plays a significant role in Waldorf education, and Rudolf Steiner emphasized its importance in the development and well-being of children. Some of the impacts of rhythm on children, as per Steiner's teachings:

1. **Sense of Security:** Rhythms in daily, weekly, and seasonal activities create a sense of predictability and stability for children. Knowing what to expect and when helps them feel secure in their environment, reducing anxiety and promoting emotional well-being.

2. **Regulation of Energy:** Rhythms help children regulate their energy levels throughout the day. Steiner observed that children have natural rhythms of rest and activity, and aligning the school day with these rhythms allows them to engage fully during active times and rest and rejuvenate during quiet times.

3. **Sense of Order and Discipline:** Rhythms provide a framework for daily life, instilling a sense of order and discipline. Children develop self-discipline when they know what is expected of them and when, leading to a more harmonious learning environment.

4. **Support for Learning:** Steiner believed that specific subjects and activities are best introduced during particular stages of child development. Following a rhythmic curriculum allows teachers to present age-appropriate content, supporting the child's learning and understanding.

5. **Connection to Nature:** Waldorf education values the connection to the natural world. Rhythms that align with the changing seasons and natural cycles help children develop a deeper appreciation and understanding of nature.

6. **Social Cohesion:** Group activities and rituals, such as morning circle or seasonal festivals, create a sense of togetherness and social cohesion. Children learn to cooperate, respect others, and work together as they participate in these shared experiences.

7. **Holistic Development:** Rhythmic activities that involve movement, artistic expression, and storytelling engage different aspects of a child's being – physical, emotional, and intellectual. This holistic approach supports balanced development.

8. **Cultivation of Patience and Resilience:** Rhythms often require waiting, patience, and repetition. Through these experiences, children learn to cultivate patience and resilience, important qualities for future learning and life challenges.

9. **Enhanced Creativity:** Steiner believed that creativity is enhanced when children have the opportunity to alternate between periods of active engagement and quiet reflection. Rhythmic activities facilitate this balance and support creative expression.

10. **Health and Well-Being:** According to Steiner, following natural rhythms, such as sleeping and waking with the rising and setting of the sun, contributes to overall health and well-being. Rhythms that respect the body's natural cycles can lead to improved physical health.

In Waldorf education, teachers carefully structure the daily and yearly rhythms to align with the child's developmental stages, supporting their growth, learning, and overall happiness. By integrating rhythm into all aspects of school life, children are offered an enriching and nurturing environment that fosters their physical, emotional, and intellectual development.

Have you heard of Circadian Rhythms?

Circadian rhythms are natural, internal processes that regulate the sleep-wake cycle and repeat roughly every 24 hours. These rhythms are influenced by external cues, primarily light and darkness, and play a crucial role in determining our patterns of wakefulness and sleep. The term "circadian" comes from the Latin words "circa" (meaning "around") and "diem" (meaning "day"), highlighting the approximately 24-hour cycle.

Key features of circadian rhythms include:

1. **Sleep-Wake Cycle:** The most well-known circadian rhythm is the sleep-wake cycle. Our bodies are naturally inclined to be awake during daylight hours and to sleep during the night.

2. **Body Temperature:** Body temperature follows a circadian rhythm, typically peaking in the late afternoon and reaching its lowest point during the early morning hours.

3. **Hormone Production:** Various hormones, such as melatonin and cortisol, are regulated by circadian rhythms. Melatonin, often referred to as the "sleep hormone," increases in the evening to promote sleep, while cortisol, associated with wakefulness, peaks in the early morning.

4. **Cellular Repair and Metabolism:** Circadian rhythms influence cellular repair processes and metabolic functions. Certain activities, like cell division and DNA repair, are more active at specific times of the day.

5. **Mood and Cognitive Performance:** Circadian rhythms can impact mood, alertness, and cognitive performance. Disruptions to these rhythms, such as those caused by irregular sleep patterns or shift work, may lead to difficulties in concentration and mood disorders.

The body's internal circadian clock, often referred to as the "biological clock," is primarily located in the suprachiasmatic nucleus (SCN) of the brain's hypothalamus. This clock is synchronized with external cues, particularly light exposure, to ensure alignment with the natural day-night cycle.

Maintaining a consistent sleep-wake schedule and exposure to natural light during the day can help regulate circadian rhythms, promoting overall well-being and optimizing various physiological functions. Disruptions to circadian rhythms, such as those experienced during jet lag or shift work, can have temporary effects on sleep patterns, alertness, and overall health.

How circadian rhythms and Waldorf education can be linked?

- **Respect for Natural Rhythms:** Circadian rhythms highlight the importance of aligning daily activities with natural cycles. Similarly, Waldorf education respects the natural rhythms of childhood, allowing for a balanced integration of academic, artistic, and practical activities.

- **Emphasis on Sleep and Well-being:** Circadian rhythms emphasize the significance of quality sleep for overall well-being. Waldorf education recognizes the importance of a nurturing environment, including healthy sleep patterns, to support a child's physical and emotional development.

- **Outdoor Activities and Light Exposure:** Circadian rhythms are influenced by exposure to natural light. Waldorf education often encourages outdoor activities and exposure to natural light, contributing to a child's overall vitality and potentially supporting healthy circadian rhythms.

- **Holistic Development:** Waldorf education's holistic approach considers the interconnectedness of various developmental aspects, mirroring the integrated nature of circadian rhythms in regulating multiple physiological processes.

While Waldorf education doesn't specifically speak circadian rhythms, its holistic principles align with creating an environment that supports a child's overall well-being, potentially contributing to healthy sleep patterns and daily rhythms.

Kim John Payne, emphasizes the importance of rhythm in family life and education. He is particularly known for his book "Simplicity Parenting," where he discusses the significance of rhythm in supporting the well-being of children. The Key Points that Kim John Payne makes about rhythm:

1. **Creating Calm and Predictability:** According to Payne, rhythm brings a sense of calm and predictability to a child's life. Establishing daily and weekly rhythms, such as consistent mealtimes and bedtime routines, provides a comforting structure for children, reducing anxiety and promoting a feeling of security.

2. **Supporting Social and Emotional Development:** Payne believes that rhythm helps children develop a sense of belonging and connection within the family. Shared activities and rituals create a sense of togetherness, strengthening family bonds and fostering emotional well-being.

3. **Reducing Overwhelm:** In today's fast-paced world, children can easily become overwhelmed by an abundance of choices and activities. Payne suggests that simplifying a child's life through a predictable rhythm can help reduce stress and overwhelm, allowing them to focus on meaningful experiences and connections.

4. **Encouraging Focus and Attention:** Rhythm supports the development of concentration and focus in children. When they know what to expect and have a sense of order in their environment, they can engage more fully in their activities and learning.

5. **Balancing Activity and Rest:** Payne emphasizes the importance of balancing active and restful periods in a child's day. Regular breaks and downtime allow children to recharge, process their experiences, and engage in creative play.

6. **Fostering Independence and Responsibility:** By establishing consistent rhythms, children develop a sense of responsibility and ownership over their daily routines. They can gradually take on more tasks independently, building life skills and self-confidence.

7. **Promoting Creativity and Imagination:** Payne believes that rhythm creates a fertile environment for creativity and imaginative play. Children have the space and time to explore their interests and engage in unstructured play, which is essential for their cognitive and emotional development.

8. **Adapting to Developmental Changes:** As children grow and their needs change, Payne suggests that rhythms can be adapted to accommodate these shifts. Flexibility within a structured framework allows families to respond to the evolving needs of their children.

Kim John Payne advocates for the intentional use of rhythm in family life and education to create a nurturing and supportive environment for children. By incorporating rhythm into daily routines and activities, parents and educators can help children thrive emotionally, socially, and academically.

Rituals in Waldorf School

Rituals play a significant role in Waldorf education, helping to create a sense of rhythm, meaning, and connection within the school community. Rituals commonly found in Waldorf Schools: rituals commonly found in Waldorf schools:

1. **Morning Circle:** The day often begins with a morning circle where students and teachers gather to greet each other, sing songs, recite verses, and share a moment of togetherness. This ritual sets a positive tone for the day and fosters a sense of community.

2. **Seasonal Festivals:** Waldorf schools celebrate the changing seasons with festivals such as Diwali, Vishu, Holi, Gokulasthami, Raksha-Bandan. These festivals often involve artistic performances, storytelling, and rituals that connect students with the natural rhythms of the year.

3. **Birthday Celebrations:** Each child's birthday is celebrated in a special way. The birthday child may be honored with a crown, a special song, or a story. It is a time to acknowledge the uniqueness of each child and their journey of growth.

4. **Main Lesson Opening:** Before starting a new main lesson block, teachers often use a ritual or verse to signal the beginning of a new topic. This helps students transition and focus their attention on the upcoming subject.

5. **Artistic Activities:** In Waldorf education, artistic activities are an essential part of the curriculum. These activities, such as drawing, painting, knitting, and handwork, are done in a rhythmical and meditative manner, fostering creativity and artistic expression.

6. **Nature Walks:** Regular nature walks and outdoor activities are considered a ritual that connects students with the natural world and encourages a sense of wonder and reverence for nature.

7. **Storytelling:** Storytelling is an integral part of the Waldorf curriculum. Teachers often tell stories during main lessons, and students may participate in storytelling as well. The act of storytelling creates a ritualistic and engaging experience for both the teller and the listener.

8. **Closing Circle:** The day often ends with a closing circle, where students and teachers come together to reflect on the day, express gratitude, and share any highlights or challenges. This ritual provides a sense of closure and connection before heading home.

These rituals in Waldorf education serve several purposes, including fostering a sense of community, providing a structured and rhythmic environment for learning, promoting creativity and imagination, and connecting students with nature and the changing seasons. Rituals help create a sense of meaning and purpose in the daily life of the school, enriching the educational experience for students and teachers alike.

Kim John Payne emphasizes the importance of rituals in family life and parenting. He believes that rituals play a crucial role in providing stability, connection, and a sense of belonging for children.

1. **Creating Meaningful Connections:** According to Payne, rituals are moments of connection and bonding between family members. Whether it's a daily mealtime ritual, a bedtime routine,

or a special family celebration, rituals provide opportunities for families to come together, share experiences, and strengthen their relationships.

2. **Fostering Emotional Well-being:** Rituals can have a significant impact on a child's emotional well-being. They provide a sense of predictability and security, which can help reduce anxiety and create a safe space for children to express their feelings.

3. **Building Family Identity:** Through rituals, families create their unique identity and culture. These shared experiences and traditions become an essential part of a child's sense of self and belonging within the family unit.

4. **Supporting Transitions and Change:** Rituals can be especially helpful during times of transition or change, such as starting a new school year, moving to a new home, or experiencing a loss. They provide a sense of continuity and stability during these challenging times.

5. **Marking Milestones and Celebrations:** Rituals are often used to mark significant milestones and celebrations in a child's life, such as birthdays, holidays, and religious ceremonies. These rituals create cherished memories and add a sense of joy and meaning to these special occasions.

6. **Teaching Values and Cultural Heritage:** Many rituals are rooted in cultural and religious traditions, and they serve as a way to pass down values, beliefs, and cultural heritage from one generation to the next.

7. **Promoting Mindfulness and Presence:** Engaging in rituals requires presence and mindfulness. Whether it's lighting candles, saying grace before a meal, or participating in a family ritual, children learn to be present in the moment and appreciate the significance of these experiences.

8. **Creating a Sense of Order and Routine:** Rituals provide structure and order in a child's life. Regularly scheduled rituals can help children feel more secure and confident, knowing what to expect and when.

9. **Encouraging Gratitude and Appreciation:** Many rituals involve expressions of gratitude and appreciation. By practicing gratitude in rituals, children learn to be thankful for the positive aspects of their lives and develop a positive outlook.

Kim John Payne advocates for the intentional use of rituals in family life as a way to strengthen family bonds, support emotional well-being, and create a nurturing and loving environment for children to thrive. He encourages parents to be mindful of the rituals they establish and to embrace the meaningful connections they can bring to family life.

Celebrating Festivals and Seasons

Waldorf schools celebrate festivals and seasons in a way that reflects the school's values and philosophy. These celebrations are often deeply rooted in nature, the changing seasons, and cultural traditions. Some common ways Waldorf schools celebrate festivals and seasons:

1. **Seasonal Decorations:** Waldorf schools often decorate their classrooms and school spaces according to the seasons. For example, during the autumn season, they may decorate with leaves, pumpkins, and other symbols of harvest and change.

2. **Seasonal Songs and Music:** Music plays an essential role in Waldorf education, and seasonal songs and music are incorporated into daily activities and celebrations. Children may learn songs and verses that reflect the changing seasons and festivals.

3. **Nature Walks and Outdoor Activities:** Waldorf schools place a strong emphasis on connecting with nature. Students often go on nature walks to observe and appreciate the changes in the environment during different seasons.

4. **Harvest Festivals:** During the autumn season, many Waldorf schools celebrate harvest festivals, where students and their families come together to celebrate the abundance of the season. There may be performances, food, and activities related to the harvest theme.

5. **Advent Celebrations:** Advent is a special time of preparation leading up to Christmas. Waldorf schools often mark Advent with candle lighting, storytelling, and other activities that build a sense of anticipation and reflection.

6. **Winter Celebrations:** Winter solstice and Christmas are celebrated in a way that honors the inner light and the return of longer days. There may be candlelight ceremonies, songs, and storytelling.

7. **Spring Festivals:** Waldorf schools celebrate the arrival of spring with festivals that honor growth and renewal. May Day celebrations and other spring events may involve dancing, singing, and outdoor activities.

8. **Cultural Festivals:** Waldorf schools also celebrate various cultural festivals from around the world. These may include Diwali, Hanukkah, Chinese New Year, and other cultural events.

9. **Handcrafting and Art:** Students often engage in handcrafting and artistic activities related to the festivals and seasons. This may include making seasonal crafts, creating artwork, or preparing costumes for performances.

10. **Community Gatherings:** Festivals and seasonal celebrations in Waldorf schools are often community events, involving students, teachers, parents, and sometimes alumni. These gatherings foster a sense of belonging and togetherness.

In Waldorf education, celebrating festivals and seasons is not just about following customs but also about engaging the imagination, fostering a connection with nature, and nurturing a sense of wonder and reverence for the world. These celebrations play an essential role in the rhythm of the school year and contribute to the overall holistic development of the students.

Daily and Weekly Rhythms in the Classroom

In a Waldorf classroom, daily and weekly rhythms are carefully designed to create a harmonious and nurturing learning environment. Some examples of daily and weekly rhythms that you might find in a Waldorf classroom:

Daily Rhythms:

1. **Morning Circle:** The day often starts with a morning circle, where the teacher and students come together to greet each other, sing songs, recite verses, and set the tone for the day ahead.

2. **Main Lesson:** The main lesson is a dedicated block of time in the morning when students focus on a particular subject in depth. Each main lesson block typically lasts for several weeks and covers a wide range of topics, from math and language arts to history, science, and more.

3. **Outdoor Play:** Outdoor playtime is an essential part of the daily rhythm. Children have the opportunity to run, play, and connect with nature, which supports their overall well-being and development.

4. **Handwork and Creative Activities:** Waldorf classrooms often incorporate handwork, such as knitting, crochet, and sewing, into the daily schedule. Creative activities, such as drawing, painting, and modeling with beeswax, are also part of the daily rhythm.

5. **Snack and Meal Times:** Snack and meal times are moments of nourishment and social connection. In Waldorf schools, children are encouraged to eat together and share in the preparation and clean-up.

6. **Storytelling and Puppetry:** Storytelling and puppetry are important elements of a Waldorf classroom. Teachers use storytelling and puppet plays to bring subjects to life and engage the children's imaginations.

Weekly Rhythms:

1. **Painting Day:** One day a week, the students may have a dedicated painting day. They explore different painting techniques and themes to express their creativity.

2. **Eurythmy:** Eurythmy is a unique movement art in Waldorf education. It is often scheduled as a weekly activity, allowing children to explore and express themselves through movement.

3. **Foreign Language Day:** Some Waldorf schools have a foreign language day, where students immerse themselves in a foreign language through songs, games, and simple conversations.

4. **Nature Walks:** Depending on the location and setting of the school, a weekly nature walk may be scheduled. Students explore the natural world and learn about plants, animals, and seasonal changes.

5. **Music and Singing:** Music and singing are integral to the Waldorf curriculum. Students may have a designated day for music lessons, singing together, or practicing musical instruments.

These are just a few examples of the daily and weekly rhythms in a Waldorf classroom. The rhythm of the day and week helps provide a sense of stability, security, and predictability for the children, allowing them to fully engage in the learning process and develop a love for learning.

Simplifying Childhood for Balanced Growth

Slow Childhood as a Concept and its relevance

In the context of Steiner's philosophy, "Slow Childhood" refers to a conscious and intentional approach to child-rearing and education that prioritizes giving children the time and space they need to develop and grow at their own pace. The concept of Slow Childhood is inspired by the broader Slow Movement, which advocates for slowing down the pace of modern life and embracing a more mindful and deliberate way of living.

In the context of childhood, Slow Childhood emphasizes the following principles:

1. **Unstructured Play:** Slow Childhood recognizes the importance of unstructured play in a child's development. It encourages parents and educators to provide ample opportunities for children to engage in imaginative play, exploration, and creative activities without the constraints of strict schedules or adult-directed activities.

2. **Emphasis on Nature:** Slow Childhood promotes a deep connection with nature and encourages children to spend time outdoors, exploring and learning from the natural world.

Nature-based activities are seen as essential for a child's physical, emotional, and cognitive development.

3. **Limited Screen Time:** Steiner's philosophy discourages excessive use of electronic devices and screen time for young children. Slow Childhood encourages parents to limit the exposure to screens and instead focus on hands-on, real-life experiences that nurture a child's senses and imagination.

4. **Rhythm and Routine:** Slow Childhood emphasizes the importance of creating a stable and predictable rhythm in a child's daily life. Consistent routines provide children with a sense of security and help them develop a natural flow of activities throughout their day.

5. **Nurturing the Senses:** Steiner believed that early childhood is a critical period for sensory development. Slow Childhood encourages activities that stimulate all the senses, such as cooking, baking, gardening, and artistic activities.

6. **Emotional Well-being:** Slow Childhood places great importance on supporting a child's emotional well-being. It advocates for parents and educators to be present, attentive, and responsive to a child's emotional needs, providing a safe and nurturing environment for emotional growth.

7. **Holistic Education:** Steiner's educational approach is holistic, addressing the intellectual, artistic, practical, and emotional dimensions of a child's development. Slow Childhood supports an education that nourishes the whole child, fostering a love of learning and a well-rounded character.

Slow Childhood aligns with Steiner's vision of providing a gentle and nurturing environment for children, allowing them to unfold and grow naturally, free from the pressures of a fast-paced and technologically driven world. The goal is to foster healthy and balanced individuals who are in harmony with themselves, others, and the natural world.

Overstimulation of Children in Today's world

Overstimulation refers to an excessive or overwhelming amount of sensory input and external stimuli that can negatively impact a person's well-being, particularly in the context of children. Steiner believed that young children, in particular, are highly sensitive to their surroundings and can easily become overstimulated when exposed to too much noise, visual clutter, media, or fast-paced environments.

In a modern world filled with technology, screens, and constant sensory input, Steiner emphasized the importance of creating a balanced and harmonious environment for children. Overstimulation can lead to several issues, including:

1. **Emotional Imbalance:** Too much sensory input can overwhelm a child's nervous system, leading to emotional dysregulation, anxiety, and stress.

2. **Reduced Attention Span:** Overstimulation can make it difficult for children to focus and concentrate on one task or activity for an extended period.

3. **Sleep Problems:** Excessive exposure to screens and stimulating activities close to bedtime can disrupt a child's sleep patterns.

4. **Hyperactivity:** Overstimulated children may exhibit hyperactive behavior or have difficulty sitting still and engaging in quiet, calming activities.

5. **Learning Difficulties:** A constantly overstimulated environment may hinder a child's ability to absorb and process new information effectively.

To address overstimulation, Steiner's educational approach promotes creating a balanced and rhythmical environment that nurtures a child's senses and allows for periods of calm and rest.

Some strategies to prevent overstimulation in children include:

1. **Limiting Screen Time:** Minimize exposure to television, computers, and other electronic devices, especially for young children.

2. **Providing Calm Spaces:** Create designated calm and quiet spaces where children can retreat and engage in activities that promote relaxation and introspection.

3. **Sensory Awareness:** Encourage activities that engage the senses in a mindful and purposeful way, such as nature walks, artistic endeavours, and hands-on exploration.

4. **Rhythm and Routine:** Establish daily rhythms and routines that provide predictability and stability for children.

5. **Outdoor Play:** Allow ample time for outdoor play and nature exploration, which can have a grounding and calming effect on children.

By fostering a balanced and mindful environment, Steiner's philosophy seeks to promote the well-being and healthy development of children, helping them grow into emotionally resilient and self-aware individuals.

Emphasizing Slow Childhood and Reducing Overstimulation

In the context of Waldorf education, there is a strong emphasis on promoting slow childhood and reducing overstimulation to support the healthy development of children. The Waldorf approach is influenced by Rudolf Steiner's insights, and it places great importance on providing a nurturing and balanced environment for children. Waldorf education addresses slow childhood and reduces overstimulation:-

1. **Unhurried Pace:** Waldorf schools prioritize an unhurried pace of learning, allowing children to fully immerse themselves in each stage of development. There is no rush to push children into academic subjects prematurely. Instead, the focus is on age-appropriate activities that foster creativity, imagination, and hands-on learning.

2. **Minimal Use of Technology:** Waldorf education limits the use of technology, especially screens, in early childhood. This is because excessive exposure to screens can overstimulate young children and negatively impact their development. Instead, Waldorf schools encourage more direct and sensory experiences through play, arts, and crafts.

3. **Connection with Nature:** Spending time in nature is an essential part of Waldorf education. Outdoor play and nature walks provide children with opportunities to connect with the

natural world, which can have a grounding and calming effect, counteracting the overstimulation caused by urban environments and technology.

4. **Rhythm and Routine:** Waldorf schools emphasize the importance of rhythm and routine in a child's daily life. Regular daily and weekly rhythms provide a sense of predictability and security, helping to reduce anxiety and overstimulation.

5. **Emphasis on Play and Imagination:** Play is considered a fundamental aspect of childhood in Waldorf education. Through imaginative play, children can process their experiences and emotions, fostering emotional resilience and reducing stress caused by overstimulation.

6. **Artistic Activities:** Creative activities, such as drawing, painting, singing, and storytelling, are integrated into the curriculum. These activities engage a child's senses and help to balance the overstimulation that may come from excessive exposure to academic and technological demands.

7. **Emotional Well-being:** Waldorf teachers pay close attention to the emotional well-being of each child. By nurturing a positive and supportive classroom environment, teachers help reduce the stress and anxiety that can arise from overstimulation.

8. **Respect for Individual Development:** Waldorf education recognizes that each child develops at their own pace. There is no pressure to achieve specific academic milestones within a rigid timeframe, allowing children to learn at their own rhythm.

By emphasizing slow childhood and reducing overstimulation, Waldorf education aims to support children in developing their full potential physically, emotionally, and spiritually. The nurturing and holistic approach of Waldorf schools helps children grow into well-balanced, resilient individuals who are better equipped to navigate the challenges of the modern world. One practice we follow with Arnav if we travel from one city to another through Public transports over long distances, we keep the next day for Arnav as a settle in day. This has shown us results to calm him down better.

The Importance of Unstructured Play and Nature Connection

According to Steiner's teachings and Waldorf education philosophy, unstructured play and nature connection are of great importance in supporting the healthy development of children.

The Key reasons why these elements are emphasized:

1. **Development of Imagination:** Unstructured play provides children with the freedom to use their imagination and creativity. In open-ended play scenarios, children can create their own worlds, stories, and characters, which fosters cognitive and emotional development.

2. **Social Skills:** During unstructured play, children often engage in cooperative and imaginative play with their peers. This type of play helps children develop essential social skills, such as communication, negotiation, problem-solving, and empathy.

3. **Physical Development:** Unstructured play often involves physical activities such as running, jumping, climbing, and balancing. These activities contribute to the development of gross motor skills, coordination, and overall physical health.

4. **Stress Reduction:** Play, particularly outdoor play, is known to reduce stress and anxiety in children. Connecting with nature and engaging in free play provides a sense of freedom, joy, and relaxation that can counterbalance the pressures of academic and structured activities.

5. **Nature Connection:** Steiner emphasized the importance of nature in a child's development. Nature offers a rich sensory experience and opportunities for exploration. Being in natural surroundings allows children to connect with the natural world, fostering a sense of wonder, appreciation, and environmental consciousness.

6. **Balance and Grounding:** In today's fast-paced, technology-driven world, unstructured play and nature connection provide a counterbalance to overstimulation. These experiences allow children to slow down, be present in the moment, and experience a sense of grounding and connectedness.

7. **Creativity and Problem-Solving:** Unstructured play encourages children to think creatively and solve problems independently. They learn to adapt, invent, and find solutions to challenges, which are valuable skills for their future development.

8. **Resilience and Confidence:** When children engage in unstructured play and nature exploration, they encounter risks and uncertainties, which help them build resilience and self-confidence. They learn to navigate new situations and trust in their abilities.

9. **Appreciation of Simple Pleasures:** In the simplicity of unstructured play and nature exploration, children learn to

appreciate the beauty of simple pleasures and the wonders of the natural world.

In Waldorf education, unstructured play and nature connection are integrated into the daily routines and curriculum to provide children with ample opportunities for growth and development. The focus on fostering a strong connection with nature and promoting imaginative, child-led play helps children develop into well-rounded individuals with a deep sense of wonder and a lifelong love for learning and the natural world.

Balancing Technology in the Digital Age

As per Steiner's philosophy and Waldorf education principles, balancing technology in the digital age is crucial for the healthy development of children. While technology has become an integral part of modern life, it is essential to approach its use with mindfulness and consideration of its impact on children's well-being and development.

What are the key aspects of balancing technology in the digital age:

1. **Delayed Introduction:** In Waldorf education, there is an emphasis on delaying the introduction of technology to young children. Steiner believed that in the early years, children should primarily engage in real, hands-on experiences and unstructured play. The focus during these formative years is on developing their physical, emotional, and social capacities.

2. **Limiting Screen Time:** As children grow older and are introduced to technology, it is essential to set limits on screen time. Excessive screen time can interfere with healthy development and impact

a child's ability to engage in other enriching activities. Waldorf schools often limit the use of technology in the classroom and encourage parents to do the same at home.

3. **Quality over Quantity:** When technology is used, we would advocate for a focus on quality content. Educational and age-appropriate materials can be used to support learning and exploration. Additionally, technology should not replace essential human interactions and hands-on experiences.

4. **Balance with Nature and Creative Play:** To counterbalance the potential negative effects of technology, Waldorf education places a strong emphasis on nature connection and creative, imaginative play. Engaging in outdoor activities, arts, and crafts, and storytelling helps children develop a well-rounded sense of self and fosters their creativity and emotional intelligence.

5. **Modeling Healthy Tech Use:** Adults play a significant role in shaping children's relationship with technology. Modeling healthy tech use, such as setting aside designated screen-free times or engaging in meaningful activities together, helps children develop a balanced approach to technology.

6. **Mindful Use of Technology:** When technology is integrated into the educational setting, Waldorf educators are encouraged to use it mindfully and purposefully. Technology should be a tool to enhance learning and not a replacement for more fundamental learning experiences.

7. **Cultivating Critical Thinking:** As children grow older and become more exposed to technology and digital media, Waldorf education emphasizes the importance of cultivating critical

thinking skills. Children are encouraged to question, analyze, and evaluate the information they encounter online, promoting digital literacy and discernment.

8. **Encouraging Active Play and Movement:** In contrast to sedentary screen time, Waldorf education advocates for plenty of active play and movement. Physical activities and movement not only support healthy development but also provide a balance to the sedentary nature of technology use.

By finding a balance between technology and other essential aspects of a child's development, Waldorf education aims to create a nurturing and enriching environment that supports children's overall well-being and helps them grow into thoughtful, creative, and balanced individuals in the digital age.

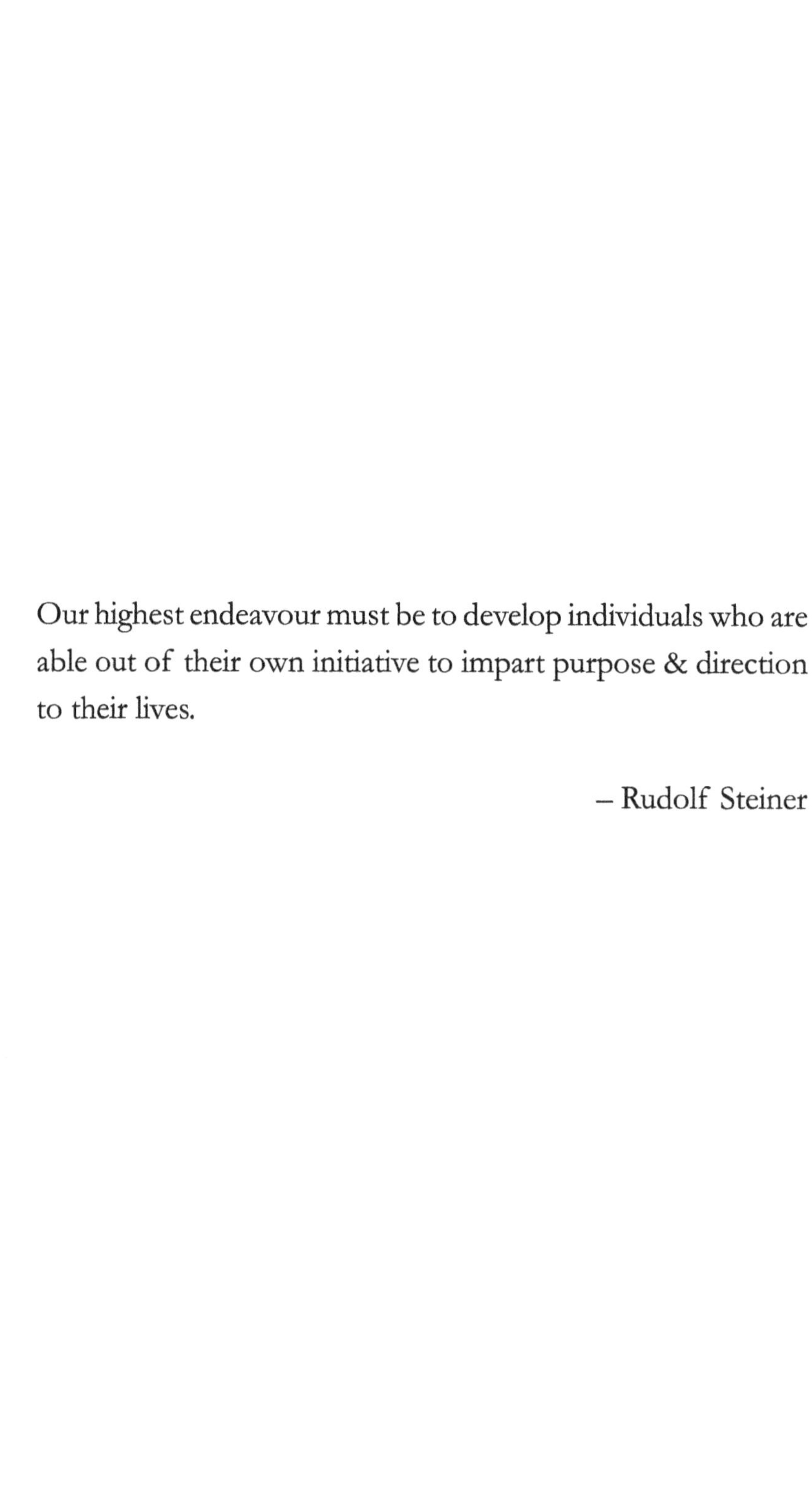
Our highest endeavour must be to develop individuals who are able out of their own initiative to impart purpose & direction to their lives.

– Rudolf Steiner

06 The Parent's Role in Waldorf Education

According to Rudolf Steiner, the process of children choosing their parents is a spiritual concept that he referred to as the "karmic relationship" between parents and children. Steiner believed in the idea of reincarnation and karma, which suggests that the soul goes through multiple lifetimes, and each lifetime is shaped by the actions and experiences of previous lives.

In this context, Steiner proposed that before incarnating into a new life, the soul of a child has a spiritual connection with the souls of its future parents. This connection is based on karmic relationships and the need for the child's soul to experience specific lessons, challenges, or opportunities in the new life that align with the parents' karma.

In other words, Steiner's belief was that children are drawn to parents whose souls can provide the necessary circumstances for the child's spiritual growth and development in the current lifetime. The choice of parents is not random but is driven by a spiritual purpose and intention.

Steiner's view on children choosing their parents emphasizes the importance of recognizing and accepting the unique individuality and spiritual journey of each child. It suggests that each child comes into the world with specific needs, challenges, and potential, and it is the role of the parents to support and guide the child on their spiritual path.

It is important to note that Steiner's views on reincarnation, karma, and the spiritual connection between parents and children are part of his anthroposophical philosophy and may not align with conventional beliefs or scientific perspectives. These ideas are foundational to Steiner's approach to education and parenting within the context of Waldorf education.

Steiner's view on the parents' role in child development emphasizes the significance of creating a balanced, nurturing, and purposeful environment that allows children to unfold their full potential and connect with their own inner wisdom. It is an approach that acknowledges the spiritual dimension of the child and aims to foster their growth as whole individuals within the context of family and community.

Key aspects of parents' role:

- **Nurturing the Child's Physical Development:** Steiner emphasized the importance of creating a nurturing and harmonious environment that supports the child's physical growth and well-being. This includes providing healthy nutrition, ample opportunities for movement and play, and ensuring a rhythm of daily activities that align with the child's natural cycles.

- **Cultivating Emotional and Social Development:** Steiner advocated for parents to be emotionally available and responsive to their children's needs. Building a strong emotional bond and fostering a sense of security helps children develop healthy self-esteem and social skills.

- **Creating a Home Environment:** Parents are encouraged to create a home environment that is aesthetically pleasing and rich in sensory experiences. A Waldorf-inspired home is often filled with natural materials, meaningful artwork, and a sense of warmth and beauty.

- **Encouraging Imagination and Creativity:** Steiner believed in the power of imagination and creativity in child development. Parents can support this by providing open-ended toys, storytelling, and engaging in artistic activities together.

- **Modeling Behavior:** Steiner emphasized that parents serve as powerful role models for their children. Parents should strive to embody the values and qualities they wish to instill in their children.

- **Emphasizing Play and Outdoor Exploration:** Parents are encouraged to prioritize unstructured play and outdoor exploration. Time spent in nature and free play allows children to connect with the natural world and fosters their sense of wonder and curiosity.

- **Balancing Media and Technology:** Steiner cautioned against excessive use of media and technology in early childhood. Instead, parents are encouraged to provide a media-free environment and offer enriching, hands-on experiences.

- **Supporting Spiritual Growth:** Steiner believed in the spiritual nature of the child and the importance of supporting their spiritual development. This involves providing opportunities for inner reflection, cultivating reverence, and acknowledging the uniqueness of each child's spiritual journey.

Becoming the First Teacher: Parent-Child Connection

Rudolf Steiner emphasized the significance of a strong and loving parent-child connection as a foundational element in child development. According to Steiner, the parent-child relationship forms the basis for the child's emotional, social, and spiritual growth. Here are some aspects of Steiner's views on parent-child connection:

1. **Unconditional Love and Acceptance:** Steiner stressed the importance of providing children with unconditional love and acceptance. Children need to feel secure and loved, knowing that their parents support them no matter what.

2. **Emotional Availability:** Parents should be emotionally available and attuned to their children's needs. This involves active listening, empathetic responses, and being present with the child during both joyful and challenging moments.

3. **Respect and Reverence:** Steiner encouraged parents to treat children with respect and reverence, recognizing their unique individuality and spiritual nature. This approach fosters a sense of dignity and self-worth in the child.

4. **Creating Rhythms and Rituals:** Establishing daily and weekly rhythms and meaningful family rituals helps children feel safe and secure. Regular routines provide a sense of predictability and comfort, supporting the child's emotional well-being.

5. **Bonding Through Play and Imagination:** Engaging in play and imaginative activities with children allows parents to form a deeper bond. Play provides an opportunity for

parents and children to connect on a joyful and creative level.

6. **Modeling Behavior:** Steiner believed that parents are powerful role models for their children. Therefore, parents should strive to embody the qualities and values they wish to instill in their children.

7. **Encouraging Independence and Autonomy:** While nurturing the parent-child connection, Steiner also recognized the importance of gradually fostering a child's independence and autonomy. Children should be given opportunities to explore and make decisions, always within a safe and supportive environment.

8. **Supporting Inner Development:** Steiner emphasized the spiritual nature of the child and the importance of supporting their inner development. Parents can provide an environment that allows for inner reflection, reverence, and connection with the child's inner world.

Steiner's approach to parent-child connection is rooted in love, respect, and understanding. It encourages parents to be actively engaged and present in their children's lives, supporting their emotional, intellectual, and spiritual growth. A strong parent-child connection not only benefits the child's development but also lays the foundation for a harmonious and nurturing family life.

Parents are considered to be the child's first and most important teachers. The philosophy is based on the idea that children learn best through imitation, and their primary source of imitation is their parents and caregivers. As mentioned above pointers show how parents become the first teacher of the child.

Waldorf education sees parents as essential partners in a child's learning journey. By being present, engaged, and responsive to the child's needs, parents become the child's first teacher and lay the foundation for a lifelong love of learning and exploration.

Supporting Children's Development at Home and School

Waldorf education emphasizes a holistic approach to supporting children's development both at home and in school. The philosophy recognizes that a child's development is interconnected with their environment and experiences.

The key aspects of how Waldorf education supports children's development at home and school:

1. **Rhythm and Routine:** Creating a consistent and predictable daily and weekly rhythm is essential for children's well-being and development. Both at home and school, Waldorf education encourages the establishment of rhythmic activities like meal times, sleep routines, and playtime, which provide a sense of security and stability for the child.

2. **Imitation and Modeling:** Waldorf educators and parents serve as positive role models for children. Children learn best through imitation, so adults' behavior, speech, and attitudes are carefully considered to foster positive qualities in the child.

3. **Nature Connection:** Waldorf education places a strong emphasis on connecting children with nature. Schools often incorporate outdoor activities, nature walks, and gardening to foster a sense of wonder and reverence for the natural world.

4. **Creative Play and Imaginative Activities:** At home and in school, children are encouraged to engage in creative and imaginative play. Waldorf classrooms are filled with natural toys and open-ended materials that stimulate the child's imagination and creativity.

5. **Artistic and Handwork Activities:** Art, music, movement, and handwork are integral parts of the Waldorf curriculum. These activities not only support children's artistic expression but also enhance their cognitive, emotional, and physical development.

6. **Minimal Use of Technology:** Waldorf education advocates for limited use of technology, especially in the early years. Both at home and in school, the focus is on fostering real-world experiences and face-to-face interactions.

7. **Nurturing Social Skills:** Social development is an essential aspect of a child's education. Waldorf schools promote an inclusive and cooperative social environment, where children learn to work together, resolve conflicts, and develop empathy.

8. **Respectful Discipline:** Discipline in Waldorf education is based on respect and understanding. Adults guide children with empathy and clear boundaries, emphasizing the importance of self-discipline and inner motivation.

9. **Celebrating Festivals and Seasons:** Waldorf schools and families often celebrate seasonal festivals and events, connecting children with cultural traditions and the rhythms of nature.

10. **Individualized Learning:** Waldorf education acknowledges that each child is unique and has their own learning pace and style.

Teachers and parents work together to provide individualized support and nurture the child's interests and strengths.

By aligning home and school environments with these principles, Waldorf education seeks to create a harmonious and nurturing context for children's growth and development. The aim is to support children in becoming well-rounded individuals with a sense of wonder, creativity, and a lifelong love of learning.

Creating a Waldorf Home Environment

Creating a Waldorf-inspired home environment involves fostering a nurturing and enriching space that aligns with the principles of Waldorf education. What are the key elements to consider:

1. **Natural and Simple Surroundings:** Use natural materials and simple designs for furniture, decorations, and toys. Opt for wooden toys, natural fabrics, and earthy colors to create a calming and soothing atmosphere.

2. **Rhythms and Daily Rituals:** Establish daily and weekly rhythms that provide predictability and stability for the child. Follow consistent meal times, bedtime routines, and other daily rituals to create a sense of security.

3. **Art and Creativity:** Encourage artistic expression and creativity in the home. Provide art supplies like watercolors, colored pencils, and modeling beeswax for the child to explore and create.

4. **Imaginative Play:** Offer open-ended toys that stimulate imaginative play. Items like play silks, wooden blocks, and dolls without fixed expressions allow children to use their imagination freely.

5. **Minimal Technology:** Limit the use of electronic devices and screen time, especially for young children. Instead, focus on real-world experiences and hands-on activities.

6. **Nature Connection:** Incorporate elements of nature in the home environment. Display seasonal crafts, bring in plants, or create a nature table to connect children with the changing seasons.

7. **Fairy Tales and Stories:** Share age-appropriate fairy tales, folktales, and stories with children. These stories nourish the child's imagination and moral development.

8. **Music and Movement:** Engage in music and movement activities with the child. Sing songs, play musical instruments, and have moments of active play.

9. **Outdoor Play:** Create opportunities for outdoor play and exploration. Have a garden or outdoor space where the child can connect with nature and engage in free play.

10. **Quiet and Calm:** Allow for periods of quiet and calm in the home. Create a cozy reading nook or space where the child can retreat and have some alone time.

11. **Parental Presence:** Be fully present with the child and engage in activities together. Quality time and meaningful interactions strengthen the parent-child bond.

12. **Respectful Discipline:** Use positive and respectful discipline strategies that focus on guiding the child's behavior with understanding and empathy (The Soul of Discipline book is a good reference point).

13. **Festivals and Celebrations:** Celebrate seasonal festivals and special occasions with simple rituals and traditions. Embrace the beauty of each season and create a sense of wonder for the child.

Remember that creating a Waldorf-inspired home environment is not about adhering to strict rules but rather about nurturing a child's sense of wonder, imagination, and connection with the world. Observe the child's interests and needs, and adapt the environment accordingly to support their development and well-being.

Sarvavyaapi Siksha

Eurythmy - The Art of Movement in Waldorf Education

Eurythmy is a form of movement therapy that was developed by Rudolf Steiner, the founder of anthroposophy. It is based on the belief that movement, gesture, and speech have a profound impact on the physical, emotional, and spiritual aspects of human beings.

In eurythmy, specific movements and gestures are used to address imbalances and disharmonies in the individual's being. These movements are derived from the sounds and rhythms of speech and music, and they are choreographed in such a way that they have a therapeutic effect on the individual.

The practice of eurythmy is highly individualized, with the therapist carefully observing and assessing the unique constitution and condition of each person. Based on this assessment, the therapist designs a customized eurythmy therapy program that is tailored to the individual's specific needs and challenges.

Eurythmy therapy can be used to address a wide range of health issues, including physical illnesses, developmental challenges, and emotional and psychological imbalances. It is also used as a preventive measure to promote overall well-being and harmony.

One of the key principles of Eurythmy therapy is the idea that movement is a reflection of the individual's inner state. By working with movement and gesture, the therapist can help the individual become more aware of their inner processes and facilitate healing and transformation.

Eurythmy therapy is often practiced in conjunction with other forms of anthroposophic medicine, including herbal remedies, nutrition, and counseling. It is typically carried out in individual or group sessions, and the individual is encouraged to actively participate in their healing process.

In addition to its therapeutic benefits, eurythmy therapy is also considered an art form, as the movements and gestures are choreographed in a way that is aesthetically pleasing and harmonious. Many people find the practice of eurythmy therapy to be deeply transformative and enriching, as it can help them connect with their inner self and find balance and healing on multiple levels.

Eurythmy therapy is a unique and holistic approach to healing that recognizes the interconnectedness of body, soul, and spirit. It offers individuals the opportunity to engage in a process of self-discovery and self-healing through movement, gesture, and artistic expression.

Let us look at the evolution of eurythmy:

1. **Origins with Rudolf Steiner:** Eurythmy was first introduced by Rudolf Steiner in 1912 as part of his anthroposophical teachings. Steiner saw eurythmy as a means to bring harmony and balance to the individual's physical, emotional, and spiritual aspects. He believed that eurythmy could be a bridge between the spiritual

world and the physical world, allowing individuals to express the spiritual impulses through movement.

2. **Early Developments:** In the early years, eurythmy was primarily used as a form of artistic expression and was performed mainly in anthroposophical communities and schools. Steiner's wife, Marie von Sivers, was instrumental in the early development and promotion of eurythmy.

3. **Therapeutic Applications:** Over time, eurythmy began to be used in therapeutic settings, particularly within the realm of anthroposophic medicine. Eurythmy therapy was developed, where specific movements and gestures were used to address physical, emotional, and psychological imbalances in individuals.

4. **Further Development and Diversification:** As eurythmy gained popularity, it started to diversify and adapt to different cultural contexts. Various eurythmy schools and training centers were established in different parts of the world, contributing to the development of different styles and approaches to eurythmy.

5. **Application in Education:** Eurythmy became an integral part of Waldorf education, which was also founded by Rudolf Steiner. In Waldorf schools, eurythmy is taught as an artistic and educational practice for students of all ages, helping to develop their physical coordination, artistic expression, and connection to language and music.

6. **Contemporary Eurythmy:** Today, eurythmy continues to thrive and evolve as an artistic and therapeutic practice. It is taught in various settings, including schools, performance groups, and therapeutic centers. There are different styles and approaches to eurythmy, each emphasizing unique aspects of the practice.

Eurythmy has evolved from its early beginnings as an artistic and spiritual expression to a diverse and multifaceted practice that encompasses both artistic and therapeutic dimensions. It continues to be embraced by individuals and communities around the world who appreciate its profound impact on personal development, well-being, and artistic expression.

The Significance of Eurythmy in Waldorf Education

Eurythmy plays a central role in Waldorf education and is considered one of the core subjects taught in Waldorf schools. It is a unique and integral part of the Waldorf curriculum, and its significance lies in its ability to address the holistic development of the child—intellectually, emotionally, and physically.

In Waldorf education, eurythmy serves several purposes:

1. **Artistic Expression:** Eurythmy is taught as an art form, similar to dance or music. Students learn various movements and gestures that are choreographed to correspond with speech, music, and poetry. It is a form of embodied poetry, where the sounds and rhythms of language and music are brought to life through movement.

2. **Connection to Language and Music:** Eurythmy helps students develop a deeper connection to language and music. Through eurythmy, children learn to understand and express the rhythms, sounds, and meaning of language and music in a physical and artistic way.

3. **Physical Coordination:** Eurythmy exercises involve precise movements and coordination of the body. It helps children

develop balance, spatial awareness, and fine motor skills, fostering a sense of grace and poise in their movements.

4. **Emotional Expression:** Eurythmy encourages children to express their emotions through movement. It provides a creative outlet for children to express their feelings and experiences in a non-verbal way.

5. **Social Integration:** Eurythmy is often practiced in groups, promoting a sense of cooperation and social integration among students. It fosters a sense of community and harmony within the class.

6. **Therapeutic Benefits:** Eurythmy is also used in Waldorf schools for therapeutic purposes. Eurythmy therapy can be beneficial for children with specific physical or emotional challenges, helping them to find balance and healing through movement.

Eurythmy is introduced to children at a young age in Waldorf education and continues throughout the primary and high school years. In the early years, eurythmy focuses on playful and imaginative movements that are developmentally appropriate for young children. As students' progress through the grades, eurythmy becomes more complex, with movements becoming more refined and connected to the curriculum themes and subjects.

Eurythmy in Waldorf education is a powerful and enriching practice that supports children's artistic expression, physical development, emotional well-being, and connection to language and music. It fosters a deep appreciation for movement as a means of artistic and personal expression, contributing to the overall balanced and holistic education provided by Waldorf schools.

The Practice of Eurythmy

In Waldorf schools, Eurythmy is practiced regularly as part of the curriculum. It is typically taught as a separate subject and is integrated into the daily rhythm of the school. What are some aspects of the practise of eurythmy in Waldorf schools:

1. **Frequency and Duration:** Eurythmy is usually taught several times a week, with each session lasting around 30 to 45 minutes. In the early years, eurythmy may be shorter and more play-based, gradually becoming more structured and formal as students progress through the grades.

2. **Age-Appropriate Movements:** Eurythmy lessons are designed to be developmentally appropriate for the age of the students. In the early years, the movements are often based on imaginative play and simple rhythmic exercises. As students get older, the movements become more complex and are connected to the curriculum themes and subjects.

3. **Artistic Expression:** Eurythmy is taught as an art form, similar to dance or music. Students learn specific movements and gestures that correspond with sounds, speech, music, and poetry. They work with the rhythms and sounds of language and music to create artistic and meaningful movements.

4. **Group Practice:** Eurythmy is usually practiced in groups, fostering a sense of cooperation and social integration among students. Group eurythmy exercises often involve coordination and synchronization among the participants.

5. **Eurythmy Performances:** In addition to regular eurythmy lessons, Waldorf schools often organize eurythmy performances and presentations. Students may perform eurythmy pieces for parents, teachers, and the wider school community as part of school events and festivals.

6. **Therapeutic Applications:** Eurythmy is also used for therapeutic purposes in Waldorf education. Eurythmy therapy is offered to students who may benefit from its healing and balancing effects. Eurythmy therapists work with individual students to address specific physical, emotional, or developmental challenges.

7. **Integration with the Curriculum:** Eurythmy is integrated into the overall curriculum of the school, complementing and enhancing other subjects. For example, eurythmy movements may reflect themes from language arts, science, history, or music lessons.

8. **Cultural and Seasonal Celebrations:** Eurythmy is often an integral part of cultural and seasonal celebrations in Waldorf schools. Students may perform eurythmy pieces during festivals, assemblies, and other special events.

Eurythmy is valued as an essential part of the Waldorf education, promoting artistic expression, physical development, emotional well-being, and social integration. It enriches the overall educational experience for students, fostering creativity, movement, and a deep appreciation for the arts.

Eurythmy's Therapeutic Benefits

Eurythmy, both as a form of artistic expression and as a therapeutic modality, offers various benefits for individuals. In the context of eurythmy therapy, it is believed to have the following therapeutic benefits:

1. **Physical Benefits:** Eurythmy exercises involve specific movements and gestures that can help improve coordination, balance, and flexibility. It can support the development of fine and gross motor skills, leading to increased physical well-being.

2. **Emotional Regulation:** Eurythmy encourages mindful movement and self-awareness, which can be beneficial for emotional regulation. Through eurythmy therapy, individuals may learn to express and process emotions in a healthy and constructive way.

3. **Stress Reduction:** Engaging in eurythmy can promote relaxation and stress reduction. The rhythmic and flowing movements, coupled with a focus on breathing, can help individuals release tension and find inner calm.

4. **Enhanced Concentration and Focus:** Eurythmy requires concentration and attention to detail. Practicing eurythmy regularly can improve focus and attention, which can be particularly helpful for individuals with attention difficulties.

5. **Support for Specific Conditions:** Eurythmy therapy is often tailored to address specific conditions or challenges. It can be used to support individuals with developmental delays, learning difficulties, and various physical or emotional ailments.

6. **Integration of Body, Soul, and Spirit:** Eurythmy is based on the concept that movement, sound, and soul qualities are interconnected. Through eurythmy therapy, individuals can experience a sense of harmony and integration of body, soul, and spirit.

7. **Improved Body Awareness:** Eurythmy exercises encourage individuals to become more aware of their bodies and movement patterns. This heightened body awareness can lead to better posture and overall body alignment.

8. **Enhanced Social Skills:** Eurythmy therapy often involves group exercises, which can foster social interaction and cooperation. It can be particularly beneficial for individuals who struggle with social skills or have difficulties relating to others.

9. **Encouragement of Creativity:** Eurythmy therapy involves creative expression through movement. This can inspire individuals to explore their creativity and develop a deeper connection with their own artistic potential.

10. **Support for Overall Well-Being:** Eurythmy therapy is a holistic approach that considers the individual's physical, emotional, and spiritual well-being. It aims to support the whole person and promote overall health and balance.

It is essential to note that eurythmy therapy is often practiced under the guidance of trained eurythmy therapists who tailor the exercises to meet the specific needs of each individual. The therapeutic benefits of eurythmy can vary depending on the individual's condition, receptivity to the therapy, and the skill of the therapist in creating a supportive and healing environment.

Fostering Creativity and Self-Expression through Eurythmy

Eurythmy, as an expressive and artistic movement form, has a profound impact on fostering creativity and self-expression in individuals. Here are some ways in which eurythmy nurtures creativity and self-expression:

1. **Freedom of Movement:** Eurythmy allows individuals to explore movement in a free and artistic manner. Participants are encouraged to move with creativity and imagination, expressing themselves through gestures, shapes, and patterns.

2. **Integration of Art and Movement:** Eurythmy combines artistic elements, such as music and poetry, with movement. This integration of art forms provides a unique opportunity for individuals to express themselves artistically and emotionally through their bodies.

3. **Inner Experience to Outer Expression:** Eurythmy focuses on the inner experience of movement and its connection to emotions and soul qualities. This process of inner exploration leads to authentic and heartfelt expressions in the outer movements.

4. **Nonverbal Communication:** Eurythmy is a form of nonverbal communication that allows individuals to convey feelings, thoughts, and ideas without using words. It provides an alternative means of expression, especially for those who may find it challenging to express themselves verbally.

5. **Improvisation and Spontaneity:** Eurythmy often includes improvisation exercises, where individuals are encouraged to create movements spontaneously. This fosters a sense of playfulness and allows for unrestricted creative expression.

6. **Group Interaction and Collaboration:** Eurythmy is often practiced in groups, promoting collaboration and collective creativity. Participants work together to create harmonious and synchronized movements, fostering a sense of unity and interconnectedness.

7. **Encouragement of Individuality:** Eurythmy celebrates individuality and uniqueness. Participants are encouraged to express themselves in their distinct ways, allowing for a diverse range of creative expressions.

8. **Embodiment of Inner Qualities:** Eurythmy enables individuals to embody various inner qualities and soul gestures, such as joy, sadness, courage, and grace. Through movement, they can externalize and give form to their inner experiences.

9. **Deepening Artistic Sensibilities:** Engaging in eurythmy deepens one's artistic sensibilities and appreciation for the aesthetics of movement. This newfound sensitivity to artistic expression can extend to other forms of art and creative endeavors.

10. **Empowerment and Confidence:** As individuals gain confidence in their ability to express themselves creatively through eurythmy, it can positively impact their self-esteem and overall sense of empowerment.

Eurythmy provides a safe and nurturing space for individuals to explore and develop their creative potential. Whether practiced as a performing art or as a therapeutic modality, eurythmy offers a rich and transformative experience that supports the blossoming of creativity and self-expression in individuals of all ages.

Eurythmy as a Social Art

Eurythmy as a social art is its practice in schools, particularly in Waldorf education. In Waldorf schools, eurythmy is often integrated into the curriculum and becomes an integral part of the students' daily experiences.

Eurythmy functions as a social art in the school setting:-

1. **Group Eurythmy Classes:** Eurythmy is taught in group classes, where students come together to learn and practice the art form. Through these classes, students not only learn the movements and gestures but also develop a sense of cooperation and collaboration with their peers.

2. **Classroom Performances:** Students often perform eurythmy pieces in front of their classmates or during school assemblies. These performances encourage students to work together as a team, supporting and complementing each other's movements to create a harmonious and aesthetically pleasing experience.

3. **Eurythmy Festivals:** In some Waldorf schools, eurythmy festivals or performances are organized where students from different classes or age groups come together to showcase their eurythmy skills. These festivals promote a sense of community and shared artistic expression among students, teachers, and parents.

4. **Eurythmy with Teachers and Parents:** Eurythmy is not limited to students; teachers and parents are also encouraged to participate in eurythmy classes and performances. This inclusion creates a sense of unity and shared experience among the entire school community.

5. **Social Interaction during Practices:** During eurythmy practices, students interact with each other, observing and supporting their peers' movements. This fosters a sense of empathy and understanding as they learn to respond to each other's cues and create a cohesive group performance.

6. **Eurythmy in Festivals and Celebrations:** Eurythmy performances often feature prominently in school festivals, seasonal celebrations, and cultural events. These performances become a way for the school community to come together and share in the artistic expression of the students.

7. **Collaborative Eurythmy Projects:** In some schools, eurythmy may be incorporated into interdisciplinary projects where students work together with their teachers to create performances related to specific subjects or themes. This collaborative approach encourages teamwork and creativity.

8. **Community Outreach:** Some Waldorf schools organize eurythmy performances for the wider community, inviting parents, friends, and members of the neighborhood to attend. These events not only showcase the students' artistic talents but also strengthen the school's connection with the broader community.

Through these various examples, eurythmy serves as a social art that brings individuals together, promotes cooperation, communication, and empathy, and fosters a sense of unity and shared artistic experience within the school community. It demonstrates how art can become a vehicle for social transformation and community building, aligning with the principles of Waldorf education and Rudolf Steiner's vision for holistic human development.

Eurythmy is not only a form of artistic expression but also a social art that brings people together in a harmonious and cooperative way. As a social art, eurythmy emphasizes the following aspects:

1. **Group Collaboration:** Eurythmy is often performed in groups or ensembles, requiring participants to work together in harmony. Each individual's movements contribute to the overall beauty and coherence of the performance, emphasizing the importance of cooperation and collective effort.

2. **Communication and Interaction:** Eurythmy is a nonverbal art form that relies on gestures, movements, and spatial relationships to convey emotions, ideas, and themes. Through these nonverbal expressions, eurythmists communicate and interact with one another, fostering a deep sense of connection and understanding.

3. **Listening and Responsiveness:** Eurythmy requires participants to be attentive and responsive to each other's movements. They must listen to the rhythm, pace, and intentions of their fellow eurythmists to maintain synchronicity and unity in the performance.

4. **Empathy and Empowerment:** Eurythmy encourages empathy as participants attune themselves to the emotional and artistic expressions of others. By recognizing and affirming each other's contributions, participants feel empowered and valued within the group.

5. **Cultural Diversity:** Eurythmy is practiced in various parts of the world, reflecting cultural diversity. As a social art, it brings people from different backgrounds together, promoting cultural exchange, appreciation, and mutual respect.

6. **Conflict Resolution:** Within the context of eurythmy, conflicts may arise during group practice or rehearsals. Addressing these conflicts requires open communication, negotiation, and a shared commitment to finding solutions, promoting skills that extend beyond the art form.

7. **Community Building:** Eurythmy performances often engage wider communities, fostering a sense of belonging and unity among participants and spectators alike. The art form's inclusive nature helps build and strengthen social bonds.

8. **Celebration of Individuality:** While eurythmy emphasizes group collaboration, it also celebrates the uniqueness of each participant. Individuality is encouraged, allowing eurythmists to bring their personal qualities and artistic expressions to the collective endeavor.

9. **Shared Aesthetic Experience:** As eurythmists move in harmony, they create a shared aesthetic experience that can evoke deep emotional responses and inspire a sense of beauty and wonder among both performers and audiences.

10. **Social Transformation:** Beyond the artistic aspects, eurythmy as a social art has the potential to contribute to broader social transformation. Through its emphasis on cooperation, empathy, and shared creativity, eurythmy fosters values and qualities that can positively impact relationships and communities.

Eurythmy is not merely a physical expression of movement but a social art that brings people together, fostering cooperation, communication, empathy, and celebration of individuality. By engaging in eurythmy, participants experience the transformative power of art in creating harmonious and interconnected social experiences.

Eurythmy Beyond the Classroom

Eurythmy beyond the Classroom refers to the application and practice of eurythmy outside of the traditional educational setting, extending its benefits and artistic expression to various other areas of life. Eurythmy, as a form of movement art, has the potential to enrich and enhance different aspects of human experience beyond the boundaries of the classroom. How eurythmy can be applied beyond the classroom:

1. **Therapeutic Settings:** Eurythmy is widely used as a therapeutic modality, known as eurythmy therapy. Trained eurythmy therapists work with individuals of all ages, including children, adults, and the elderly, to address various physical, emotional, and mental health concerns. The therapeutic movements of eurythmy are tailored to meet the specific needs of each individual, promoting balance and well-being.

2. **Performing Arts and Theatre:** Eurythmy is often incorporated into theatrical performances and artistic productions. Professional eurythmists collaborate with actors, dancers, musicians, and other artists to create multidisciplinary performances that combine movement, music, and speech.

3. **Social and Community Events:** Eurythmy performances and workshops can be featured in community events, cultural gatherings, and festivals. Eurythmy groups may share their artistic expressions with the wider community, enriching the overall cultural landscape.

4. **Corporate Settings:** Some organizations and companies integrate eurythmy workshops or movement exercises into their employee wellness programs. Eurythmy can help employees enhance their creativity, reduce stress, and improve communication and teamwork.

5. **Therapeutic Eurythmy for Special Needs:** Eurythmy can be adapted and used for individuals with special needs, providing them with a creative and therapeutic outlet for self-expression and well-being.

6. **Mindfulness and Meditation:** The rhythmic and harmonious movements of eurythmy can be utilized in mindfulness practices and meditation, promoting inner stillness and self-awareness.

7. **Cultural and Educational Events:** Eurythmy performances may be featured in cultural and educational events, contributing to the celebration of diversity and artistic expression.

8. **Personal Practice and Self-Development:** Eurythmy can also be practiced individually as a form of personal movement meditation and self-development.

Eurythmy beyond the Classroom demonstrates the versatility and adaptability of eurythmy as an art form and therapeutic practice. It expands the scope of eurythmy beyond its educational context, showcasing its potential to enrich various aspects of human life, promote well-being, and contribute to a more vibrant and harmonious society.

Man is a form proceeding out of movement. Eurythmy is a continuation of divine movement, of the divine form in man. By means of Eurythmy man approaches nearer the divine than he otherwise could.

– Rudolf Steiner

Embracing Diverse Learners (SPD, ADHD)

Welcome to the fascinating world of sensory integration, where the development of your child's senses unfolds like an enchanting story. As parents and educators, we often encounter children whose behaviours puzzle us. Consider these scenarios:

- Rohan, who covers his ears during group singing.

- Neha, the child who enjoys rolling on the floor while others sit in circle time.

- Aarushi, who hesitates to touch playdough, sand, or paint.

- Kartik, the fearless climber who scales tables and takes daring leaps.

- Riya, the spirited child who frequently stumbles and ends up with scraped knees.

- Aryan, who prefers not to engage with outdoor playground activities.

These children, and many more like them, might be grappling with sensory integration challenges. Sensory integration is like a finely orchestrated symphony within their central nervous system, playing a crucial role in how they perceive and interact with their surroundings.

Just as our rich Indian traditions and culture embrace our five fundamental senses of touch, sight, hearing, taste, and smell, we delve deeper into the comprehensive framework of twelve senses, as illuminated by Steiner. But that's not all. We'll also uncover the lesser-known senses, such as the vestibular sense, which governs movement and balance, and the proprioceptive sense, which provides an awareness of body position.

Together, these senses guide a child's development, aiding their journey from bewildering infancy to active childhood. As parents, educators, and caregivers, it's our responsibility to nurture and support these senses, ensuring that they flourish harmoniously.

Sarvavyaapi Siksha is your awareness guide through this profound journey. Within its pages, you'll find insights into recognizing, understanding, and empowering children as they traverse their unique sensory paths. By nurturing holistic growth and addressing sensory integration, we empower our children to flourish not only academically but as well-rounded individuals, deeply rooted in our cultural heritage.

So, let's embark on this enlightening journey through the world of sensory integration. Along the way, we'll simplify the complex and provide engaging insights to make the journey both enjoyable and enriching.

A remarkable figure in the field of sensory integration, Dr. A. Jean Ayres, was an occupational therapist and educational psychologist who made significant contributions in the mid-1900s. She studied sensory integration and introduced the concept of sensory integration dysfunction. In 1973, she authored the groundbreaking book, "Sensory Integration and Learning Disorders," which laid the foundation for understanding and addressing sensory integration issues in children.

Dr. Ayres developed assessment tools to identify sensory integration dysfunction and trained many occupational therapists in assessing and treating children facing such challenges. Her Sensory Integration Theory continues to be the cornerstone for assessing and helping children with sensory integration problems.

Building on Dr. Ayres' work, many occupational therapists, along with parents and educators, have taken up the cause of diagnosing and treating sensory integration issues. The book "The Out-of-Sync Child: Recognizing and Coping with Sensory Processing Disorder" by Carol Kranowitz, published in 2006, has played a vital role in raising awareness about how sensory processing difficulties can affect young children's daily lives, including those in early childhood education.

Sensory Processing Disorder (SPD) is a condition where individuals struggle to effectively use sensory information gathered from their senses like sight, hearing, touch, taste, smell, movement, and body awareness in their daily lives. Most people are naturally skilled at taking in sensory cues, making sense of them, and reacting appropriately. For instance, if you smell cookies burning in the oven, see smoke, and hear the oven timer, you would likely head to the kitchen to remove the cookies from the oven. This is how your brain processes sensory information, integrating inputs from your nose, eyes, and ears into an effective response.

However, SPD arises when someone's brain doesn't properly organize these sensory signals, resulting in an ineffective response. To illustrate, in the cookie-burning scenario, an individual with SPD might react by covering their ears and yelling, which is a disorganized and unhelpful response, making it challenging for them to function effectively in their environment.

Sensory processing disorders (SPDs) are when the way your brain handles what you feel, hear, see, smell, or taste doesn't work as it should. It can affect one sense or more than one. Sometimes, it affects all of them.

Imagine your brain is like a message center, and it gets lots of messages from your body. These messages tell your brain how things feel, sound, look, smell, or taste. It's what makes you enjoy a hug, feel happy eating your favorite food, or pull your hand away from something hot.

Now, think about what happens when someone's message center doesn't work properly. They might not enjoy good sensations, like a gentle touch or a nice smell. They might even scream or get really upset from things that aren't usually a big deal, like leaves rustling or clothes feeling uncomfortable.

On the other hand, some people might not notice dangerous or bad things, like getting hurt or feeling too hot or cold.

SPDs have three main types:

1. **Sensory Modulation Disorder:** This is when people have trouble dealing with sensations. They might be too sensitive and get upset easily, or they might not feel things when they should.

2. **Sensory-Based Motor Disorder:** This affects how they move. They might have trouble balancing, moving, or using their hands the right way.

3. **Sensory Discrimination Disorder (SDD):** This makes it hard to understand sensations. For example, they might not know how to handle something gently, so they break it. Or they could have a tough time finding their way when walking.

Each of these types can have even more specific kinds of problems, but these are the main things to know about sensory processing disorders.

Type of SPD	Subtype	Description and Examples
Sensory Modulation Disorder	Over-Responsivity (Hyperresponsiveness)	• Difficulty handling sensory input. - Examples: Can't stand vacuum cleaner noise or reacts strongly to light touch.
	Under-Responsivity (Hypo-responsiveness)	• Difficulty registering sensory input. - Examples: Doesn't notice when they're dirty or wet after eating.
Sensory-Based Motor Disorder	Poor Balance	• Difficulty with balance and spatial orientation. - Examples: Frequent tripping, struggles with activities like riding a bike.
	Difficulty with Motor Coordination	• Challenges with fine motor skills. - Examples: Struggles to tie shoelaces, button a shirt, or use scissors.
	Awkward Movements	• Lack of coordination in gross motor skills. - Examples: Bumps into objects, difficulty with dancing or sports.
Sensory Discrimination Disorder (SDD)	Tactile Discrimination Issues	• Difficulty recognizing tactile sensations. - Examples: Struggles to hold delicate objects without breaking them.
	Visual Discrimination Issues	• Difficulty distinguishing visual input. - Examples: Confusion between similar-looking letters or objects.
	Proprioceptive Discrimination Issues	• Challenges in understanding body positioning. - Examples: Difficulty knowing how much to bend the elbow while eating.

Children and adults with SPD may exhibit a range of symptoms, including:

- Difficulty with transitions and changes in routine
- Overreacting or underreacting to sensory stimuli
- Poor coordination and motor skills
- Impulsivity or difficulty with self-regulation
- Avoidance of certain sensory experiences
- Delayed speech and language development
- Trouble with fine motor tasks, such as handwriting
- Challenges with social interactions and play

SPD can co-occur with other conditions, such as autism spectrum disorder, attention deficit hyperactivity disorder (ADHD), and developmental delays. It is essential for individuals with suspected SPD to be evaluated by occupational therapists or other qualified professionals who specialize in sensory integration to determine an appropriate treatment plan.

Vestibular issues are a common feature of Sensory Processing Disorder (SPD) in children. The vestibular system is responsible for processing sensory information related to balance, spatial orientation, and movement. When there are vestibular processing issues, a child may struggle to make sense of the sensory input related to movement and balance, leading to various challenges in their daily life.

Children with vestibular issues may exhibit the following signs and symptoms:

1. **Poor Balance:** They may have difficulty maintaining balance when sitting, standing, or walking. They may appear clumsy or unsteady.

2. **Motion Sensitivity:** They may be sensitive to movement, such as getting car sick easily or feeling uncomfortable on swings or playground equipment.

3. **Fear of Heights or Movement:** They may avoid activities that involve heights or rapid movement, such as climbing or riding a bike.

4. **Delayed Motor Milestones:** Children with vestibular issues may achieve motor milestones, such as crawling, walking, or running, later than their peers.

5. **Poor Coordination:** They may struggle with coordinating movements, leading to challenges in sports and physical activities.

6. **Difficulty Modulating Movement:** They may have difficulty controlling the force and speed of their movements, leading to issues with handwriting and other fine motor tasks.

7. **Sensory Seeking or Avoiding Behaviors:** Some children with vestibular issues may seek out intense movement experiences, while others may avoid them altogether.

It's important to note that vestibular issues can vary in severity and may co-occur with other sensory processing challenges. Early identification and intervention are essential for supporting children with SPD and vestibular issues in their development and improving their functional abilities and overall well-being. Parents, teachers, and caregivers play a crucial role in understanding and accommodating the child's sensory needs to create a supportive and enriching environment.

Occupational therapists specializing in sensory integration can assess and provide intervention for children with vestibular issues. Therapy may involve activities that provide controlled movement experiences, such as swinging, spinning, or rocking, to help the child's vestibular system become more regulated and better integrated with other sensory systems.

Occupational therapy is a common intervention for individuals with SPD, aimed at helping them develop better sensory processing and integration skills. Therapy may involve various sensory activities and exercises to improve the individual's response to sensory input and enhance their overall daily functioning. With the right support and understanding, individuals with SPD can learn to navigate their sensory challenges and improve their quality of life.

Identifying Sensory Processing Disorder (SPD) at home can be challenging, but there are certain signs and behaviors that may indicate a child is experiencing sensory processing difficulties. It's important to remember that every child is unique, and not all signs will be present in every child. If you suspect your child may have SPD, it is best to consult with a developmental pediatrician or an occupational therapist specializing in sensory integration for a comprehensive evaluation.

Some common signs of SPD that you may observe at home:

1. **Over-Reactivity to Sensory Input:** The child may show extreme reactions to sensory stimuli, such as becoming upset or overwhelmed by loud noises, bright lights, certain textures, or strong smells.

2. **Under-Reactivity to Sensory Input:** Conversely, the child may appear unresponsive to sensory stimuli and seem unaware of pain or temperature changes.

3. **Difficulty with Transitions:** The child may have trouble transitioning between activities or environments, becoming upset or anxious during changes.

4. **Poor Coordination and Balance:** The child may appear clumsy, have difficulty with activities that require coordination (e.g., catching a ball), or have a preference for sedentary activities.

5. **Sensitive to Touch:** The child may be sensitive to touch and may avoid certain textures or become upset when touched.

6. **Avoidance of Certain Foods:** The child may be a picky eater and avoid certain foods based on their textures, colors, or smells.

7. **Easily Distracted or Impulsive:** The child may have difficulty staying focused or may be impulsive in their actions.

8. **Resistance to Grooming or Dressing:** The child may resist certain grooming activities, such as hair brushing or teeth brushing, or have difficulty with dressing (e.g., sensitivity to clothing tags).

9. **Difficulty with Fine Motor Skills:** The child may struggle with tasks that require fine motor skills, such as handwriting or using scissors.

10. **Difficulty with Gross Motor Skills:** The child may have challenges with activities that involve gross motor skills, such as riding a bike or climbing stairs.

11. **Sensory Seeking Behaviors:** The child may seek out intense sensory experiences, such as crashing into furniture or spinning in circles.

If you notice several of these signs and they significantly impact the child's daily life, it may be a good idea to seek professional evaluation. An occupational therapist can conduct a thorough assessment to determine if the child has SPD and develop a personalized intervention plan to address their sensory needs. Early identification and intervention can help children with SPD improve their sensory processing abilities and enhance their overall functioning and well-being.

Arnav, a child with Sensory Processing Disorder (SPD), received occupational therapy (OT) to address his challenges in processing sensory inputs, particularly those related to movement and balance. As part of his home program, Arnav's therapy included specially designed equipment like lycra swings and ladders, which were strategically installed to provide the necessary sensory inputs. Additionally, his daily routine incorporated a strict rhythm to create a predictable and structured environment.

The OT sessions with necessary activities were carefully tailored to suit Arnav's needs and abilities. Safety and comfort were paramount, and the use of appropriate-sized equipment ensured he could engage comfortably. The lycra swings and ladders served as tools to stimulate his vestibular system, which played a significant role in improving his balance and coordination.

The benefits of this approach were evident in Arnav's progress:

1. **Regulated Sensory System:** The swinging activities and other sensory inputs provided by the lycra swings and ladders helped regulate Arnav's sensory system. They supported him in managing his sensory sensitivities, reducing feelings of anxiety, and promoting a sense of calmness.

2. **Enhanced Sensory Integration:** The rhythmic movements of the swings and the challenging tasks offered by the ladders fostered better sensory integration. As Arnav engaged in these activities regularly, his brain gradually learned to process and interpret sensory information more effectively.

3. **Improved Motor Skills:** The swinging and ladder activities required Arnav to coordinate his movements and develop his motor skills. Over time, he became more proficient in navigating the swings and maneuvering on the ladders, contributing to his overall physical development.

4. **Increased Body Awareness:** Swinging back and forth on the lycra swing and navigating the ladder required Arnav to be aware of his body in space. These activities promoted a greater sense of body awareness and spatial orientation.

5. **Consistency and Predictability:** The strict rhythm implemented in Arnav's daily routine provided him with a sense of stability and predictability. This consistent structure contributed to a more organized sensory experience, reducing sensory overload.

The home program, under the guidance of an occupational therapist, was adjusted to suit Arnav's comfort level and progress. The therapy sessions focused on gradually challenging him to further develop his sensory and motor skills while keeping the environment supportive and encouraging.

Overall, the combination of OT interventions, specialized equipment, and a structured daily rhythm played a significant role in supporting Arnav's sensory processing and self-regulation. By providing him with the right tools and environment, his therapy aimed to empower him to navigate the challenges of SPD and promote positive developmental outcomes.

We are truly grateful for the support and understanding that Arnav's school has shown regarding his SPD challenges. The Waldorf approach has given us the opportunity to focus on Arnav's unique needs and has been instrumental in helping us identify and address his SPD issues, which we might not have realized in other school settings.

The change in schools has made a significant difference in Arnav's well-being, as we have noticed a reduction in his meltdowns. The child-centered and nurturing environment at the Waldorf school has provided him with the right balance of academic learning and creative exploration, which has positively impacted his development.

It's fascinating to observe how Arnav's interests and imaginative play have flourished in this environment. Though he may sometimes imitate certain behaviors he has seen, we understand that it's not a result of exposure to such behaviors. Instead, it is likely a manifestation of how SPD influences his perception and response to the world around him.

The school's emphasis on unstructured play, nature connection, and artistic activities has been beneficial for Arnav's sensory regulation. The activities have a calming effect on him and provide a predictable and comforting environment, helping him manage his SPD challenges.

As parents, we are fully engaged in supporting Arnav's growth and development. We appreciate the open communication with his teachers, which allows us to collaborate on strategies and ensure that he receives the right support both at home and in the classroom.

Arnav's interest in imaginative play, like pretending to be a police officer, is just a natural part of his growth and development. We encourage him to explore his creativity through role-play, as it contributes positively to his emotional and social development.

The Waldorf education philosophy has truly empowered us as parents to be actively involved in Arnav's journey. We understand the importance of working closely with the school and his teachers to provide him with the best possible support.

In conclusion, we are thrilled to see the positive impact that the Waldorf school has had on Arnav's life. With the school's understanding, the right environment, and our loving support, we are confident that Arnav will continue to grow and thrive despite his SPD challenges. The foundation laid by his experiences at the Waldorf school will undoubtedly serve him well in his future endeavours. We remain deeply grateful for the positive influence of Waldorf education in our lives and in Arnav's life.

The Waldorf Approach to Inclusive Education

The Waldorf approach to inclusive education is rooted in the philosophy that every child is unique and has their own individual strengths and challenges. In a Waldorf school, inclusivity is not just a goal but an inherent part of the educational philosophy. The approach seeks to create a learning environment where all children, regardless of their abilities or backgrounds, are embraced and provided with opportunities to grow and develop to their fullest potential.

Key aspects of the Waldorf approach to inclusive education:

1. **Respect for Individual Differences:** In a Waldorf school, teachers value and respect each child's individuality. They recognize that every child learns and develops at their own pace and in their own way. This understanding allows teachers to adapt their teaching methods to meet the diverse needs of their students.

2. **Holistic Development:** The Waldorf approach focuses on the holistic development of a child, encompassing not just academic learning but also emotional, social, and artistic development. This comprehensive approach enables teachers to address the diverse needs of students across various domains.

3. **Multi-Sensory Learning:** Waldorf classrooms often incorporate multi-sensory learning experiences that cater to different learning styles and abilities. By engaging multiple senses, students with various learning needs can participate fully in the learning process.

4. **Differentiation and Individualized Instruction:** Waldorf teachers are skilled in differentiating instruction to meet the unique needs of their students. They create lesson plans that accommodate diverse learning styles and abilities, ensuring that all children can actively engage in the learning experience.

5. **Inclusive Arts and Movement:** The arts and movement play a central role in Waldorf education. These elements provide avenues for self-expression, creativity, and learning for all children, including those with diverse learning needs.

6. **Emphasis on Social and Emotional Learning:** Waldorf education places significant importance on social and emotional learning. Creating a supportive and caring classroom environment fosters a sense of community and belonging, benefiting all students, including those with social challenges.

7. **Parental Involvement and Collaboration:** Inclusive education in a Waldorf school involves collaboration between teachers, parents, and other professionals involved in a child's development. This teamwork ensures that the child's unique needs are understood and addressed effectively.

8. **Flexible Curriculum:** The Waldorf curriculum is designed to be flexible, allowing teachers to adapt and modify the learning experiences to suit the needs of each child. This flexibility enables all students to actively participate and learn at their own pace.

9. **Teacher Training and Professional Development:** Waldorf teachers undergo extensive training that equips them with the skills to support and accommodate diverse learning needs. Ongoing professional development ensures that teachers remain updated on best practices in inclusive education.

Inclusivity for special needs children is an essential aspect of the Waldorf approach to education. Waldorf schools strive to create a welcoming and supportive environment where children with special needs are embraced, respected, and provided with the necessary support to participate fully in the educational journey alongside their peers.

Key aspects of inclusivity for special needs children in Waldorf schools:

- **Individualized Support:** Waldorf schools recognize that each child with special needs has unique challenges and strengths. Teachers work closely with parents, specialists, and therapists to develop individualized education plans that address the specific needs of the child. This personalized approach ensures that children receive the support and accommodations they require to thrive in the classroom.

- **Adaptive Learning Materials:** Waldorf teachers are skilled at creating and adapting learning materials to suit the needs of all students, including those with special needs. They use various tools and techniques to make the curriculum accessible and engaging for every child, regardless of their abilities.

- **Inclusive Arts and Movement:** The arts and movement play a central role in Waldorf education, and they are particularly beneficial for special needs children. Creative expression through art, music, drama, and movement allows children to communicate, engage, and learn in ways that are meaningful to them.

- **Emphasis on Social Skills:** Inclusivity in a Waldorf school extends beyond academic support. Teachers focus on fostering social skills and emotional intelligence in all students, including those with special needs. Creating a caring and compassionate classroom community helps children develop social connections and a sense of belonging.

- **Collaboration and Teamwork:** Inclusivity for special needs children requires collaboration between teachers, parents, therapists, and other professionals. Waldorf schools encourage open communication and teamwork to ensure that the child's needs are understood and addressed comprehensively.

- **Celebrating Diversity:** Waldorf schools celebrate diversity and recognize that every child has unique gifts to offer. By valuing and appreciating the differences among students, the school community becomes a place of acceptance and understanding.

- **Sensory Integration:** Waldorf classrooms are designed to be sensory-rich environments that accommodate different sensory needs. Children with sensory processing challenges benefit from the calming and stimulating elements incorporated into the learning environment.

- **Holistic Approach:** The Waldorf approach takes into account the whole child, including their physical, emotional, and spiritual well-being. Special needs children receive support not just in academics but also in developing life skills and self-confidence.

- **Parental Involvement:** Inclusivity for special needs children is strengthened by active parental involvement. Parents are encouraged to share their insights and experiences to help create the best possible learning environment for their child.

Waldorf schools are committed to providing an inclusive education that honors the individuality of every child, including those with special needs. Through personalized support, adaptive teaching methods, and a nurturing environment, special needs children in Waldorf schools are empowered to discover their potential, cultivate their strengths, and develop a deep love for learning. The inclusive spirit of Waldorf education extends a warm embrace to all children, fostering an environment of acceptance, growth, and joy in the pursuit of knowledge.

The Waldorf approach to inclusive education is grounded in the belief that every child deserves an education that nurtures their individuality and encourages their unique gifts. By creating an inclusive and nurturing learning environment, Waldorf schools aim to support the growth and development of all children, fostering a sense of belonging and enabling them to thrive academically, emotionally, and socially.

Sensory Processing Disorder (SPD) is an essential consideration in the context of inclusive education, and it is crucial to acknowledge and address the unique challenges that children with SPD may face in the classroom. In Waldorf schools that prioritize inclusivity, the needs of children with SPD are taken into account to ensure that they can fully participate in the educational experience.

SPD affects how the brain processes and responds to sensory information, and it can lead to difficulties in processing everyday stimuli like touch, sound, taste, smell, and movement.

In a Waldorf classroom, the following strategies and accommodations are employed to support children:

1. **Sensory-Friendly Environment:** Waldorf schools often create sensory-friendly classrooms that consider lighting, sound levels, and seating arrangements to accommodate the sensory needs of all students, including those with SPD.

2. **Sensory Breaks:** Teachers may allow sensory breaks for children with SPD, providing them with opportunities to self-regulate and refocus when sensory input becomes overwhelming.

3. **Flexible Seating:** Providing flexible seating options, such as wobble stools or floor cushions, allows children with SPD to choose seating that best suits their sensory preferences and needs.

4. **Visual Aids:** Visual schedules and cue cards can help children with SPD understand and navigate daily routines, reducing anxiety and promoting independence.

5. **Fidget Tools:** Some children with SPD benefit from fidget tools or manipulatives that can help them maintain focus and manage sensory input during lessons.

6. **Reducing Overstimulation:** Teachers in Waldorf schools may create a calming and predictable atmosphere by minimizing excessive noise, distractions, and sudden transitions.

7. **Occupational Therapy (OT) Support:** Collaborating with occupational therapists, Waldorf schools may incorporate OT techniques and exercises into the daily routine to support children with SPD.

8. **Encouraging Self-Advocacy:** Teachers work with children to develop self-awareness and self-advocacy skills, empowering them to express their sensory needs and preferences.

9. **Supportive Staff Training:** Teachers and staff receive training and professional development to better understand SPD and provide appropriate support and accommodations.

10. **Parent Involvement:** Parents play a vital role in advocating for their child's needs and providing valuable insights to help the school create a supportive learning environment.

By actively addressing SPD and implementing supportive strategies, Waldorf schools can ensure that children with SPD are valued members of the school community, where their unique strengths and challenges are acknowledged and embraced. Inclusive education in a Waldorf setting promotes a sense of belonging and fosters the child's overall well-being, enabling them to flourish academically, socially, and emotionally.

Understanding ADHD

ADHD stands for Attention Deficit Hyperactivity Disorder. It is a neurodevelopmental disorder that typically begins in childhood and affects a person's ability to pay attention, control impulsive behaviors, and regulate hyperactivity. ADHD is a complex condition, and its exact cause is not fully understood. However, researchers believe that it is likely to be caused by a combination of genetic, environmental, and neurological factors.

1. **Genetics:** There is evidence to suggest that ADHD can run in families. If a parent or sibling has ADHD, the likelihood of a child developing the disorder increases.

2. **Brain Chemistry and Structure:** Studies have shown that people with ADHD may have imbalances in certain brain chemicals (neurotransmitters) that are involved in attention and impulse control, such as dopamine and norepinephrine. Additionally, some brain imaging studies have revealed differences in brain structure and activity in individuals with ADHD.

3. **Environmental Factors:** Certain environmental factors may contribute to the development of ADHD. These can include exposure to toxins during pregnancy, premature birth, low birth weight, and prenatal substance use.

4. **Brain Injury or Damage:** In some cases, brain injuries or damage to specific areas of the brain can lead to symptoms that resemble ADHD.

5. **Maternal Smoking and Alcohol Use:** Some research suggests that maternal smoking during pregnancy and alcohol use may increase the risk of ADHD in children.

It is important to note that ADHD is not caused by poor parenting or excessive sugar consumption, as was once believed. It is a complex neurological condition that requires a comprehensive approach to diagnosis and treatment.

While the exact cause of ADHD may not be known, early identification and appropriate intervention can significantly improve outcomes for children with the disorder. If parents suspect that their child may have ADHD, it is essential to seek a comprehensive evaluation from a qualified healthcare professional or a child psychologist. Proper diagnosis and early intervention can lead to effective management strategies and support to help children with ADHD reach their full potential.

ADHD (Attention Deficit Hyperactivity Disorder) is associated with differences in brain functioning, which can be observed through brain imaging studies. These differences in brain activity and structure are believed to contribute to the symptoms of ADHD, such as inattention, hyperactivity, and impulsivity. Few aspects of brain functioning that are relevant to ADHD:

1. **Frontal Lobes:** The frontal lobes of the brain are responsible for executive functions, including attention, self-control, and planning. In individuals with ADHD, there may be differences in the development and functioning of the frontal lobes, leading to challenges in focusing attention and inhibiting impulsive behaviors.

2. **Neurotransmitters:** Neurotransmitters are chemicals that transmit signals between brain cells. In individuals with ADHD,

there may be imbalances in certain neurotransmitters, such as dopamine and norepinephrine, which play a crucial role in regulating attention and behavior.

3. **Default Mode Network (DMN):** The DMN is a network of brain regions that are active when the mind is at rest or not engaged in specific tasks. In individuals with ADHD, there may be atypical patterns of activity within the DMN, which could contribute to difficulties in sustaining attention.

4. **Reward System:** The brain's reward system involves the release of dopamine in response to positive experiences. In individuals with ADHD, there may be differences in how the brain responds to rewards, which could influence motivation and attention.

5. **Cerebellum:** The cerebellum is involved in motor control and coordination, but it also plays a role in cognitive functions, including attention and working memory. Differences in cerebellar function have been observed in individuals with ADHD.

It's important to note that while brain functioning differences are associated with ADHD, they are not the sole cause of the disorder. ADHD is a complex condition with multiple contributing factors, including genetic, environmental, and neurological factors. The brain differences observed in individuals with ADHD are not a result of personal choice or behavior but rather reflect the underlying neurological basis of the disorder.

Understanding the brain functioning aspects related to ADHD can help researchers and clinicians develop more targeted interventions and treatments to support individuals with ADHD in managing their symptoms and improving their daily functioning. Early intervention and appropriate support can make a significant difference in helping individuals with ADHD lead fulfilling and successful lives.

Rudolf Steiner did not specifically address ADHD as it is understood today, as the concept of ADHD was not recognized during his time. Steiner's educational philosophy, focuses on the holistic development of children, emphasizing the balance of intellectual, emotional, and physical aspects of the child.

While Steiner's writings and teachings do not directly mention ADHD, some aspects of Waldorf education may be beneficial for children who struggle with attention and hyperactivity. For example:

1. **Rhythmic Structure:** Waldorf schools often follow a daily and weekly rhythm, providing predictability and routine, which can be helpful for children who thrive in structured environments.

2. **Hands-on Learning:** Waldorf education emphasizes experiential learning and incorporates arts and movement into lessons. This approach may engage children with ADHD, as it provides varied and interactive experiences.

3. **Outdoor Time:** Waldorf schools prioritize outdoor play and nature exploration, which can be beneficial for children with ADHD, as being in nature has been shown to reduce symptoms of hyperactivity and improve attention.

4. **Emphasis on Relationships:** Waldorf teachers strive to build strong relationships with their students, fostering a supportive and caring environment that can be particularly helpful for children with ADHD.

It's important to note that the understanding and treatment of ADHD have evolved significantly since Steiner's time, and the management of ADHD often involves a multi-faceted approach that may include educational, behavioral, and medical interventions. Parents and educators working with children with ADHD should seek guidance from professionals trained in the assessment and treatment of the disorder to provide appropriate support and interventions tailored to the individual child's needs.

How do Waldorf Schools deal with issues like ADHD & SPD?

Waldorf schools approach ADHD and SPD with a holistic and individualized approach, taking into consideration the unique needs of each child. While it is important to note that Waldorf schools are not specialized in treating specific learning or developmental disorders, they create an inclusive environment that aims to support the overall well-being and development of all children, including those with ADHD and SPD.

1. **Individualized Education Plans (IEPs):** Waldorf schools work closely with parents and caregivers to create individualized education plans for children with ADHD and SPD. These plans outline specific strategies and accommodations tailored to meet the child's needs and support their learning and social development.

2. **Inclusive Classrooms:** Waldorf classrooms are designed to be inclusive, allowing children with ADHD and SPD to learn alongside their neurotypical peers. Teachers are trained to provide support and adapt teaching methods to accommodate different learning styles.

3. **Rhythmic and Structured Environment:** The Waldorf educational approach emphasizes rhythm and structure in daily

activities, which can be beneficial for children with ADHD and SPD by providing a sense of predictability and stability.

4. **Hands-On Learning:** Waldorf education places a strong emphasis on hands-on and experiential learning, which can be engaging and beneficial for children with ADHD and SPD.

5. **Artistic Expression:** Creative and artistic activities, such as painting, music, and movement, are integrated into the curriculum. These activities can be therapeutic for children with ADHD and SPD, helping them express themselves and regulate their emotions.

6. **Outdoor and Nature Activities:** Waldorf schools often incorporate outdoor and nature-based activities, which can provide sensory experiences and opportunities for physical movement, benefiting children with SPD.

7. **Collaboration with Parents and Therapists:** Waldorf schools work closely with parents and external therapists to support children with ADHD and SPD. Open communication and collaboration ensure that the child's needs are addressed effectively.

8. **Focus on Emotional and Social Development:** Waldorf education emphasizes emotional and social development, promoting empathy, understanding, and respect among students. This focus helps create a supportive and compassionate community for all children.

It's important to remember that while Waldorf schools provide a nurturing and supportive environment, children with ADHD and SPD may require additional interventions and therapies beyond the school setting. Families may choose to work with healthcare professionals, occupational therapists, or other specialists to develop a comprehensive approach to address the specific needs of their child.

Individualized Support in the Waldorf School's Classroom

In Waldorf education, individualized support is an essential aspect of creating an inclusive and supportive learning environment for children with special needs. While Waldorf schools follow a comprehensive and holistic curriculum, they also recognize that each child is unique and may require personalized attention to thrive in the classroom.

Individualized support is provided in the Waldorf classroom for children with special needs by:

1. **Assessment and Observation:** Teachers in Waldorf schools carefully assess and observe each child's strengths, challenges, and learning styles. They pay close attention to how children respond to different teaching methods and activities.

2. **Collaboration with Parents:** Waldorf teachers work closely with parents to understand their child's needs, preferences, and any specific challenges they may be facing. Regular communication between parents and teachers helps in creating a consistent and supportive approach to the child's education.

3. **Individualized Education Plans (IEPs):** For children with special needs, Waldorf schools may develop Individualized Education Plans (IEPs) in collaboration with parents and other specialists. These plans outline specific goals, strategies, and accommodations to support the child's learning and development.

4. **Adaptations and Accommodations:** Teachers in Waldorf schools are skilled at adapting their teaching methods and materials to suit the individual needs of their students. They may use various instructional techniques, provide extra support, or modify assignments as necessary.

5. **Flexible Groupings:** Waldorf classrooms often include flexible groupings, allowing children to work in smaller groups or one-on-one with the teacher when needed. This flexibility ensures that each child receives appropriate attention and support.

6. **Emphasis on Social-Emotional Learning:** Waldorf education places significant emphasis on social-emotional learning and the development of strong interpersonal skills. This approach fosters a caring and supportive community where children with special needs feel included and valued.

7. **Sensory Integration and Movement:** For children with sensory processing challenges, Waldorf schools may incorporate sensory integration activities and movement exercises into the daily rhythm of the classroom. These activities can help regulate sensory responses and support overall well-being.

8. **Artistic Therapies:** Waldorf schools often integrate artistic therapies, such as eurythmy, music, and painting, into the curriculum. These therapies can have a therapeutic effect and support children in their emotional and cognitive development.

9. **Outdoor Education:** Nature-based and outdoor activities are integral to Waldorf education. For some children with special needs, spending time in nature can be calming and provide a conducive environment for learning.

10. **Professional Development:** Waldorf schools invest in ongoing professional development for their teachers, which includes training on supporting children with diverse learning needs. This ensures that teachers are equipped with the knowledge and skills to address a wide range of challenges.

By providing individualized support, Waldorf schools aim to create a nurturing and enriching educational environment where children with special needs can flourish and reach their full potential. Kindly be advised that certain Waldorf schools may face constraints in accommodating specific special needs. In the event that you are cognizant of any challenges your child may have, we encourage you to openly communicate and discuss these matters with the admission counselor or management during the admission process. This proactive dialogue ensures that the school is well-informed and equipped to address individual needs appropriately.

Nurturing Individuality in Exceptional Learners (ASD, Autism)

In the enchanting realm of education, where every child is akin to a unique bloom, there exists a profound journey of understanding and embracing individuality. "Nurturing Individuality in Exceptional Learners unfolds as a guiding beacon in this exploration, delving into the distinctive world of learners). As we embark on this transformative odyssey, we find ourselves at the intersection of compassion, knowledge, and the unwavering commitment to foster the holistic growth of every extraordinary learner.

Autism, with its spectrum of nuances, challenges the conventional norms of education, demanding a nuanced approach that recognizes and celebrates the diversity within each learner. This chapter, a tapestry woven with insights and wisdom, aims to be a source of guidance for parents to understand the intricate landscapes of Autism. It is not a chapter on strategies, narratives but an awareness attempt to create an empathetic understanding which can be designed to nurture the individuality of learners traversing the spectrum.

As we progress through this literary journey, the book Sarvavyaapi Siksha has unfolded a treasure trove of awareness & practical strategies and innovative strategies that Waldorf education unleashes. Sarvavyaapi Siksha aspires to be more than a awareness guide it strives to be a companion, offering solace and insights, this chapter is an awareness creation attempt to those traversing the labyrinth of educating exceptional learners & how early awareness can create a huge impact. This book is a testament to the belief that, with the awareness of right tools tools and understanding, every learner, irrespective of where they fall on the spectrum, can blossom into their full potential.

In this chapter Nurturing Individuality in Exceptional Learners, we invite you to embark on a voyage of empathy, enlightenment, and empowerment.

Autism Spectrum Disorder (ASD) is a neurodevelopmental disorder that affects communication, social interaction, behavior, and sensory processing. It is called a "spectrum" disorder because it can manifest in a wide range of symptoms and severity levels. Individuals with ASD may have challenges in various areas of development but can also possess unique strengths and abilities.

Common characteristics of Autism Spectrum Disorder include:

1. **Communication Difficulties:** People with ASD may have difficulty understanding and using verbal and nonverbal communication, such as gestures, facial expressions, and tone of voice. Some individuals may have limited or repetitive speech, while others may be nonverbal.

2. **Social Challenges:** Individuals with ASD often have difficulty understanding social cues, such as reading others' emotions or maintaining eye contact. They may struggle to engage in reciprocal social interactions and have difficulty forming friendships.

3. **Repetitive Behaviors:** Repetitive movements, such as hand-flapping or rocking, and repetitive interests or routines are

common in individuals with ASD. They may become upset if their routines are disrupted.

4. **Sensory Sensitivities:** People with ASD may experience heightened or diminished sensitivity to sensory stimuli, such as lights, sounds, textures, or smells. This can lead to sensory overload or withdrawal in certain environments.

5. **Special Interests:** Many individuals with ASD develop intense interests in specific topics, often focusing on one subject in great depth.

6. **Challenges with Change:** Difficulty adapting to changes in routines or new environments is common in individuals with ASD.

7. **Different Learning Styles:** Some individuals with ASD may have exceptional skills in areas such as mathematics, music, or art, while facing challenges in other academic or adaptive areas.

It is important to note that every individual with ASD is unique, and not all individuals will exhibit all the above characteristics. The severity of symptoms can vary widely, and some individuals with ASD may have exceptional strengths and talents.

The exact cause of Autism Spectrum Disorder is not fully understood, but it is believed to involve a combination of genetic and environmental factors. Early intervention and tailored support can significantly improve the quality of life for individuals with ASD, helping them develop their strengths and navigate challenges effectively. ASD is a lifelong condition, but with appropriate support and understanding, individuals with ASD can lead fulfilling lives and make meaningful contributions to society.

Autism was first identified and described by Austrian psychiatrist and physician Dr. Leo Kanner in 1943. Dr. Kanner published a seminal paper titled "Autistic Disturbances of Affective Contact" in which he detailed the case histories of 11 children who displayed similar patterns of behavior and social communication difficulties. He used the term "early infantile autism" to describe this condition.

Around the same time, a German psychiatrist named Hans Asperger was independently studying a group of children who exhibited similar behavioral characteristics, which later became known as Asperger's Syndrome, another form of autism. Asperger's work was initially conducted in the 1930s, but his findings were not widely known outside of Germany until much later.

Both Leo Kanner and Hans Asperger made significant contributions to the understanding of autism, and their work laid the foundation for further research and development of support services for individuals on the autism spectrum. Today, autism is recognized as a complex spectrum disorder, and its diagnosis and treatment have evolved considerably since its initial identification.

Recognizing signs of autism can be crucial for early intervention and support. Some common signs and behaviors often associated with autism spectrum disorder (ASD):

1. **Social Challenges:**

   ○ Difficulty making eye contact

   ○ Limited interest in or difficulty with social interactions

   ○ Trouble understanding or responding to social cues and nonverbal communication

   ○ Difficulty forming and maintaining friendships

2. **Communication Difficulties:**

   o Delayed or limited speech and language development

   o Difficulty initiating or sustaining conversations

   o Repetitive use of language or echolalia (repeating words or phrases)

   o Challenges with understanding humor, sarcasm, or figurative language

3. **Repetitive Behaviors:**

   o Engaging in repetitive body movements like hand-flapping, rocking, or spinning

   o Insistence on sameness and routines; resistance to changes

   o Preoccupation with specific interests or topics

   o Unusual sensory behaviors, such as sensitivity to lights, sounds, textures, or smells

4. **Social-Emotional Differences:**

   o Challenges with understanding and expressing emotions

   o Difficulty with empathy and recognizing others' feelings

   o Unusual emotional reactions, such as intense emotional outbursts or apparent lack of emotional response

5. **Lack of Imaginative Play:**

   o Difficulty with pretend play and imaginative activities

   o Limited creativity in play and rigid adherence to routines and rituals

It's important to note that the signs and symptoms of autism can vary widely from person to person, and some individuals may display only a few of these characteristics. Additionally, the severity of these behaviors can range from mild to severe. If you have concerns about a child's development, it's advisable to consult with a healthcare professional or specialist for a comprehensive evaluation and diagnosis. Early intervention services can make a significant difference in the lives of children with autism.

Rudolf Steiner did not specifically address autism in his teachings, as the concept of autism as a clinical diagnosis was not well-defined during his time. Steiner's work primarily focused on child development and education, and he emphasized the importance of meeting each child's individual needs and fostering a holistic approach to learning. Steiner however has done lectures on Curative Education. Curative education are lectures given to doctors and curative teachers which number of fertile suggestions for the treatment of children with special needs, it is an educational approach that is inclusive and aims to address the individual needs of children with a wide range of developmental and learning differences.

The key aspects of curative education in the context of autism:

1. **Holistic Approach:** Curative education takes a holistic approach to the development of children with special needs. It recognizes that each child is unique and seeks to address their physical, emotional, cognitive, and social development.

2. **Individualized Support:** Children with autism often have diverse strengths and challenges. Curative education places a strong emphasis on individualized support, tailoring the curriculum and teaching methods to meet each child's specific needs.

3. **Therapeutic Elements:** Curative education incorporates therapeutic elements, including art, music, movement, and eurythmy, to support children with autism. These therapies are

integrated into the educational curriculum to promote sensory integration and emotional well-being.

4. **Structured Routines:** Children with autism often benefit from structured routines and predictability. Curative education provides a structured and rhythmic daily schedule that helps children with autism feel secure and supported.

5. **Inclusivity:** Curative education emphasizes the importance of an inclusive environment. Children with autism are encouraged to be active members of the classroom community, participating in a supportive and accepting social environment.

6. **Teacher-Student Relationships:** The relationsh`ip between teachers and students is a fundamental aspect of curative education. Teachers build close, caring relationships with their students, providing emotional support and guidance.

7. **Parent Involvement:** Curative education encourages parents to be actively involved in their child's education. Parents and teachers collaborate to create a supportive home and school environment.

It's important to note that curative education is a comprehensive approach that can benefit children with autism by focusing on their overall well-being and development. The combination of educational and therapeutic elements can help children with autism reach their full potential and lead fulfilling lives.

Waldorf School Inclusivity Approach

Waldorf schools are known for their inclusive approach to education and their commitment to meeting the individual needs of each child.

Many Waldorf schools strive to create a supportive and nurturing environment for children with autism spectrum disorder (ASD).

Waldorf schools typically have small class sizes and a low student-to-teacher ratio, which allows for more individualized attention and support for children with special needs. Teachers in Waldorf schools are encouraged to be flexible and responsive to the unique learning styles and challenges of each student, including those with autism.

In Waldorf classrooms, there is a focus on experiential and hands-on learning, which can be particularly beneficial for children with autism who may have sensory processing differences. The use of art, movement, and music in the curriculum can also provide alternative means of expression and communication for children with autism.

Additionally, Waldorf schools often prioritize creating a calm and rhythmical learning environment, which can help children with autism feel more secure and regulated. Daily and weekly rhythms in the classroom can provide a sense of predictability and structure, which can be comforting for children with autism who may struggle with transitions and changes in routine.

It is important to note that each Waldorf school is unique, and the level of support and accommodations for children with autism may vary from one school to another. Some Waldorf schools may have specialized programs or additional resources to support children with autism, while others may work closely with parents and professionals to develop individualized learning plans.

The philosophy of Waldorf education aligns with principles of inclusivity and personalized learning, making it a potentially supportive and enriching environment for children with autism.

However, it is essential for parents of children with autism to visit and assess individual Waldorf schools to determine if they can meet the specific needs of their child. Collaboration and communication between parents, teachers, and professionals are crucial in ensuring that children with autism thrive in any educational setting.

Inclusivity of Autistic Children in Waldorf School: -

In Waldorf schools, there is a strong emphasis on embracing the individuality of each child. Waldorf education recognizes that every child has unique strengths, challenges, and learning styles, and seeks to create an environment that nurtures and supports the whole child.

Some ways in which Waldorf schools embrace the individuality of autistic children:

1. **Small Class Sizes:** Waldorf schools typically have small class sizes, which allows teachers to get to know each child on a personal level. This enables teachers to understand the specific needs and strengths of autistic children and tailor their approach accordingly.

2. **Individualized Support:** Waldorf teachers are trained to be observant and responsive to the needs of each child. They work closely with parents and professionals to develop individualized learning plans and accommodations that best support the autistic child's learning and well-being.

3. **Sensory-Friendly Environment:** Waldorf schools often create a sensory-friendly learning environment that considers the sensory needs of all children, including those with autism. Calm and natural surroundings, soft lighting, and limited use of screens can help create a more comfortable space for autistic children.

4. **Inclusive Arts and Movement:** Waldorf education places a strong emphasis on arts and movement as integral parts of the curriculum. These expressive forms provide alternative means of communication and engagement for autistic children, allowing them to express themselves in ways that may be more comfortable for them.

5. **Rhythm and Routine:** Consistent daily and weekly rhythms in the classroom can be beneficial for autistic children who thrive on predictability and structure. These rhythms help create a sense of safety and security in the learning environment.

6. **Social Skills Development:** Waldorf schools provide opportunities for social interaction and collaboration, helping autistic children develop social skills and build meaningful relationships with their peers.

7. **Holistic Approach:** Waldorf education takes a holistic approach to learning, addressing the intellectual, emotional, physical, and spiritual aspects of each child. This approach recognizes the interconnectedness of all aspects of development and seeks to support the whole child.

8. **Inclusive Community:** Waldorf schools foster a sense of community and acceptance among students, teachers, and parents. Autistic children are welcomed and valued as integral members of the school community.

By embracing the individuality of autistic children and providing a supportive and inclusive learning environment, Waldorf schools aim to help these children thrive and reach their full potential. It is essential to remember that each child with autism is unique, and the level of support needed may vary. Collaboration between parents, teachers, and professionals is essential in ensuring that autistic children receive the personalized care and education they require.

Disclaimer: Sarvavyaapi Siksha wishes to clarify that there are a limited number of Waldorf schools in India with trained curative education teachers. It is strongly advised to verify this information with the respective Waldorf school for accurate guidance.

Please be aware that we are not medical professionals or specialists in the aforementioned field. The above last two chapters are written to create awareness and in most cases may demand particular attention from qualified specialists and doctors for accurate diagnosis and treatment. Our efforts in this book are based on extensive reading and research, and we do not endorse or propose any specific treatments. It is crucial to consult with doctors for personalized guidance before making decisions regarding your child's well-being, as you, as the parent, are the best advocate, evaluator, and custodian for them. We assume no responsibility for any actions taken by you. We also encourage you to avoid labeling the child and maintain an awareness that each child is on a unique journey, having chosen their parents for support in their distinctive life path. Our sole intention is to promote awareness.

When human beings meet together seeking the spirit with unity of purpose then they will also find their way to each other.

– Rudolf Steiner

Influence of Family on Child Development & The Impact of Waldorf Education on Family Life and Values

In the tapestry of a child's life, family and environment are threads woven deep, shaping their values, aspirations, and the path they tread. Childhood, like an absorbing canvas, captures the essence of surroundings and family dynamics. This narrative dives into the profound impact of family life and environment on a child's growth, using stories of young minds navigating the nuances of Indian households and landscapes.

1. Family life forms the bedrock of a child's emotional development. The relationships nurtured within the family are the first chords in a symphony of empathy, trust, and emotional intelligence. Sara's story reveals how a nurturing family environment can set the stage for emotional maturity.

   Sara's parents, Ramesh and Priya, believed in open communication, empathy, and active listening. Their home resonated with love and affection, where Sara felt valued and heard. Growing up in such an environment, Sara found it natural to build deep and meaningful relationships. She cultivated empathy and compassion, becoming an emotionally intelligent individual, all thanks to the nurturing relationships she found at home.

2. Family life also molds a child's value system. Children keenly observe the beliefs and principles upheld by their families, which become their guiding stars. Alex's story underscores the influence of family values and community engagement.

Alex's parents, Anjali and Arvind, were passionate about community service. They often engaged in local charity work, taking young Alex along. These experiences imprinted upon him the importance of kindness and giving back. As he grew, these values became his own. Alex embraced community service, a testament to the impact of a values-driven family environment.

A child's cognitive development and educational journey are profoundly influenced by their immediate environment. A stimulating environment can ignite a lifelong love for learning. Maya's story is a testament to the power of a rich learning atmosphere.

Maya's parents, Manoj and Kavita, were ardent believers in holistic education. Their home was a treasure trove of books, art, and intellectual discussions. Family trips to museums, encouragement to explore art forms, and lively debates formed an integral part of Maya's upbringing. These experiences kindled her curiosity and laid the foundation for academic excellence.

The natural surroundings in which a child grows can significantly impact their development. Exposure to nature fosters a deep connection to the environment and promotes physical and mental well-being. Lia's story paints a vivid picture of the influence of the natural world.

Lia's early years were spent in a rural setting, surrounded by lush forests and sprawling meadows. His childhood was a tapestry of outdoor adventures, from hiking through dense woods to gazing at stars on clear nights. These experiences instilled in him a deep love for nature and nurtured robust physical and mental health. Liam's story exemplifies how the natural environment can cultivate a child's affinity for the outdoors and a healthy lifestyle.

Family life and environment are powerful forces shaping a child's growth. The stories of Sara, Alex, Maya, and Liam illustrate the various facets of this influence. From emotional intelligence to values, learning, and a connection to nature, every aspect of their development is intricately woven with their family life and surroundings.

In the heart of rural India, Rahul's story unfolded—a tale of dreams turned to despair. Rahul, a bright and spirited young boy, lived with his parents, Priya and Ashok, in a modest household. As he embarked on his educational journey, Rahul's aspirations were boundless, fueled by his parents' encouragement.

For many years, Priya and Ashok had toiled as agricultural laborers, enduring the harsh realities of rural life. Their deep-seated desire was to provide a brighter future for Rahul through education. They believed that education would be the ladder he needed to escape the vicious cycle of poverty and build a successful life.

Rahul thrived academically, consistently ranking at the top of his class. His parents, despite their meager income, made considerable sacrifices to ensure Rahul had access to books, tuition, and a supportive environment. They envisioned a future where their son would break free from the limitations of their own lives.

But as Rahul neared the end of his school years, his family faced mounting financial pressures. A severe drought had plagued their region, affecting crop yields and diminishing their income. Rahul's parents could no longer afford his college education, and their dreams began to crumble.

In the bustling lanes of an urban Indian neighborhood, Ananya's tale unraveled—a story shadowed by familial discord. Ananya was born into a joint family, where generations coexisted under one roof. Her grandparents, parents, uncles, aunts, and cousins shared the same home.

As she grew, Ananya was witness to simmering tensions and disagreements between her elders. The discord often reached a crescendo, making her home environment tense and hostile. The family rifts affected Ananya deeply, taking a toll on her emotional well-being and affecting her studies.

Ananya's parents, Meera and Sunil, were caught in the crossfire of the family's disputes. They struggled to provide a harmonious atmosphere for their daughter, but the relentless feuds of the joint family overwhelmed their efforts. Ananya's academic performance plummeted, and her once-bright future became clouded by stress and anxiety.

Amidst the crowded streets of a metropolitan city of India, Arjun's story was one of neglect and abandonment. Arjun's parents, Jaya and Ravi, were engrossed in their demanding careers, leaving their son to the care of nannies and daycare centers from a tender age.

Jaya and Ravi were driven by ambitions to achieve financial success, but in their pursuit, they unintentionally distanced themselves from their child. The absence of parental guidance and emotional connection left Arjun feeling isolated and unimportant. His academic performance suffered as he grappled with loneliness and a lack of support.

As Arjun grew older, he yearned for his parents' attention and guidance, but their commitments continued to consume their time. His future prospects began to dim, and his sense of direction waned.

In these stories, we glimpse the heart-wrenching consequences of negative family influence on a child's future. Rahul's dreams were thwarted by financial constraints, Ananya's potential was stifled by family feuds, and Arjun's prospects were dimmed by parental neglect.

The impact of family life on a child's development cannot be overstated. A nurturing, supportive family environment can be the catalyst for a child's success, while discord, financial strain, or parental neglect can shroud a child's future in darkness.

In the intricate fabric of Indian society, these stories serve as reminders that family dynamics and influences play pivotal roles in a child's life, shaping their journey into adulthood. The path to a brighter future is often carved by the positive guidance and support a child receives from their family.

Waldorf education is not just about the child; it's about transforming the entire family's approach to life and learning. By embracing the Waldorf philosophy and involving themselves actively in their child's education, parents become co-creators of a nurturing, holistic environment where the child can flourish emotionally, intellectually, and spiritually. It's a profound shift in mindset that transcends academics and becomes a way of life, ultimately shaping the child's future in a deeply meaningful way. Waldorf education has a holistic influence on family dynamics, impacting various aspects of family life and interactions. How Waldorf education can influence and enrich family dynamics: Waldorf education can influence and enrich family dynamics:

1. **Shared Values and Beliefs:** Families who choose Waldorf education often share common values and beliefs related to child development, creativity, nature, and the importance of a holistic education. This shared understanding creates a strong foundation for family life and decision-making.

2. **Emphasis on Rhythm and Routine:** Waldorf education encourages daily and weekly rhythms, which can extend to family life. Having predictable routines can create a sense of security and stability for children and parents alike.

3. **Connection to Nature:** Waldorf education promotes a deep connection to nature, and families often engage in outdoor activities together, fostering a love for the natural world and a sense of wonder.

4. **Artistic and Creative Expression:** Families may integrate artistic and creative activities into their daily lives, such as drawing, painting, storytelling, and music, inspired by the Waldorf curriculum.

5. **Screen-Free Time:** Waldorf education advocates limited use of screens, which can lead to more meaningful family interactions and quality time spent together without digital distractions.

6. **Parent-Child Bond:** By involving parents in their child's education, Waldorf schools strengthen the parent-child bond. Parents become more engaged in their child's learning journey, fostering open communication and understanding.

7. **Encouragement of Play:** Families are encouraged to provide unstructured playtime for children, allowing them to explore and learn freely, which can lead to more relaxed and joyful family interactions.

8. **Family Involvement in School Activities:** Waldorf schools often engage parents in school events and festivals, bringing families together to celebrate and build a sense of community.

9. **Modeling Lifelong Learning:** Through their engagement with their child's education, parents often become lifelong learners themselves, exploring new ideas and practices that benefit the entire family.

10. **Emphasis on Emotional Intelligence:** Waldorf education emphasizes emotional intelligence, which can lead to more empathetic and understanding family relationships.

11. **Focus on Imagination and Creativity:** Families may engage in imaginative play and creative projects together, stimulating the imagination and fostering a sense of wonder in both children and parents.

12. **Cultivating a Love for Learning:** Waldorf education aims to cultivate a love for learning in children, inspiring a curiosity for knowledge that extends to family life and encourages parents to explore new subjects and interests.

Waldorf education's holistic approach can positively influence family dynamics by promoting shared values, creating meaningful connections, and fostering a sense of wonder, creativity, and togetherness. The integration of Waldorf principles into family life can lead to a more harmonious and enriched family experience.

Integrating Waldorf Values Beyond School

Integrating Waldorf values beyond school involves incorporating the principles and practices of Waldorf education into various aspects of family life and daily routines. Some ways to do so:

1. **Rhythms and Routines:** Create daily and weekly rhythms at home, such as regular mealtimes, bedtimes, and family activities. This provides a sense of stability and predictability for children, mirroring the rhythms observed in Waldorf schools.

2. **Nature Connection:** Spend time outdoors as a family, engaging in nature walks, gardening, or other outdoor activities. Encourage a reverence for nature and its cycles, just as Waldorf education does.

3. **Artistic Expression:** Incorporate artistic activities into family life, such as drawing, painting, crafts, or storytelling. Encourage creativity and imaginative play, fostering the same artistic spirit as seen in Waldorf classrooms.

4. **Screen-Free Time:** Limit screen time for both children and adults. Emphasize face-to-face interactions, conversation, and play without digital distractions.

5. **Simplicity and Minimalism:** Foster a sense of simplicity and minimalism in the home environment, focusing on quality over quantity and promoting an environment conducive to creativity and free play.

6. **Family Traditions and Festivals:** Establish family traditions and celebrate seasonal festivals together. Participate in crafting decorations or preparing meals for these occasions, just as Waldorf schools mark the changing seasons.

7. **Emotional Intelligence:** Encourage emotional intelligence and open communication within the family. Create a safe space for children to express their feelings and thoughts without judgment.

8. **Storytelling and Literature:** Read and share stories with your children regularly. Waldorf education places great importance on storytelling and the use of rich, meaningful literature.

9. **Hands-on Learning:** Engage in hands-on learning experiences and practical activities with your children. Cooking, baking, and other simple projects can be opportunities for learning and bonding.

10. **Modelling Lifelong Learning:** As parents, show an interest in learning new things and pursuing your passions. Be a role model for lifelong learning and curiosity.

11. **Encouraging Play:** Provide unstructured playtime for children, both indoors and outdoors. Allow children the freedom to explore and engage in imaginative play.

12. **Emphasis on Relationships:** Prioritize meaningful connections with family members and friends. Nurture healthy relationships and foster a sense of community within the family and beyond.

By integrating Waldorf values beyond the school setting, families can create a nurturing and enriching environment that supports the holistic development of their children. These practices not only complement Waldorf education but also contribute to a balanced and harmonious family life.

The heart of the Waldorf method is that education is an art- it must speak to the child's experience. To educate the whole child, his heart and his will must be reached, as well as the mind.

– Rudolf Steiner

Traditional Parenting vs. Waldorf Inspired Parenting

Parenting is undeniably a learned art, an intricate journey of growth and adaptation. This lifelong process involves continuous learning, as it lacks a definitive manual, and each child's uniqueness demands parents to perpetually grasp and adjust to their evolving needs, behaviours, and developmental stages.

Parenting necessitates the cultivation of nurturing skills, including active listening, empathy, and efficient communication, which are progressively developed over time. Parents often explore and adopt diverse parenting styles that may span from authoritative to permissive, fine-tuning these approaches as they gain experience and wisdom. Seeking guidance from experts, educational resources, support groups, and community experiences is a common practice among parents who recognize the value of learning from those who have navigated the complex realm of child-rearing.

As children mature, parents must skilfully adjust their parenting strategies, acknowledging that what effectively addresses the needs of a toddler may not be suitable for a teenager. Furthermore, parenting is profoundly influenced by cultural norms, generational practices, and the conscious decisions parents make about which methods to embrace or adapt based on their cultural heritage and the evolving dynamics of society. Along this journey, making mistakes and learning from them is an integral part of parental growth, as they navigate the multifaceted challenges and delights of raising children.

Establishing support networks consisting of family, friends, and knowledgeable professionals can provide invaluable insights and guidance. The art of parenting entails a harmonious blend of seeking knowledge and trusting one's parental intuition, as parents become increasingly attuned to their child's distinctive needs and cues over time. It revolves around cultivating an environment that is rich in unconditional love, respect, and unwavering support, creating the fundamental building blocks for children to flourish in the world.

The journey of parenthood is a remarkable one, marked by profound moments of joy, learning, and growth. It's a path filled with countless discoveries, both about your child and yourself. Yet, in this extraordinary journey, we are rarely explicitly told that parenting, in all its complexity, is an art to be learned.

When a child is born, we are often given guidance on the immediate needs of the baby – feeding, changing diapers, ensuring a safe sleep environment. These are the basics, the essentials. But parenting goes far beyond the basics. It's not just about keeping a child alive and healthy; it's about nurturing their growth, their minds, their hearts.

As parents, we enter this journey with the purest of intentions. We want the best for our children. We want to protect them, guide them, and see them flourish. However, despite our best intentions, we soon realize that it's not as simple as we thought. Children are not blank slates waiting for us to write upon. They are unique individuals with their own temperaments, tendencies, and preferences.

So, parenting becomes a process of adaptation. It's a journey of self-discovery as much as it is about nurturing the growth of our children. We learn about their needs, their personalities, and their love languages. We come to understand the power of patience and the significance of being present. We grasp that discipline is not about control but about guidance, that love is not just a feeling but a series of actions.

As we stumble, fall, and pick ourselves up, we gain wisdom. We discover the value of consistency, the impact of our words, and the strength of our embrace. We realize that every interaction with our child is a chance to teach, to learn, to bond.

Parenting is not a static set of rules. It's a dynamic, ever-evolving art form. Just as an artist refines their skills over a lifetime, parents continually refine their approach. We seek knowledge from books, from experts, and from fellow parents who have walked similar paths. We adapt our techniques and strategies as our children grow and change.

But alongside the learning, there's an innate sense of intuition that emerges. We begin to understand our children on an instinctual level. We can sense their moods, their needs, and their unspoken worries. This intuitive connection is a beautiful aspect of parenting, one that can't be taught in a manual.

In essence, parenting is a journey of simultaneous learning and trusting. We learn from others, from experience, from our children themselves. We trust our instincts, our love, and our enduring commitment to our children's well-being.

And through it all, we discover that while parenting is indeed an art to be learned, it's also an art that we, as parents, are uniquely qualified to create and continually refine.

Traditional parenting refers to the conventional or mainstream approach to raising children that has been prevalent in many societies for generations. It often involves a set of well-established practices, beliefs, and disciplinary methods that are passed down from one generation to the next.

Traditional parenting can vary from one culture to another but typically includes certain common elements:

Aspect of Traditional Parenting	Description
Parenting Style	Authoritarian
Discipline Methods	Punishments, including spanking, time-outs, loss of privileges
Family Dynamic	Structured and hierarchical
Roles	Clear roles for parents and children
Educational Emphasis	High value on academic achievement and career success
Focus on Obedience	Emphasizes following rules and not questioning authority
Gender Roles	May involve rigid, role-specific gender expectations
Respect for Elders	Emphasizes respect for elders and authority figures
Outcome-Oriented	Focus on raising successful and conforming members of society

It's important to note that traditional parenting practices can vary widely across cultures and regions, and what may be considered traditional in one society may differ from another.

Many parents blend traditional parenting with more contemporary or progressive approaches, taking what they find most effective from each.

Waldorf inspired parenting takes a more holistic and child-centered approach, focusing on the development of the whole child—mind, body, and spirit—within a nurturing and creative environment.

How are Traditional Parenting & Waldorf inspired Parenting are different.

Aspect of Parenting	Traditional Parenting	Waldorf Inspired Parenting
Philosophical Foundation	Adherence to societal norms	Rooted in Rudolf Steiner's Waldorf philosophy
Approach to Discipline	Often relies on punitive measures and external rules	Emphasizes creative discipline, nurturing inner qualities, and responsibility
Early Education	Prioritizes early academics, structured schedules, and standardized testing	Advocates play-based early childhood education with experiential learning and imaginative play
Technology and Media	May involve early exposure to screens and digital devices	Restricts screen time for young children, encourages creative and nature-based activities
Connection to Nature	Might not prioritize a strong connection to the natural world	Values nature immersion and deep connection with the environment
Toys and Play	Encourages a wide range of plastic toys and play involving flashing lights and sounds	Prefers simple, open-ended toys made from natural materials to stimulate imaginative play
Stress on Routine	Typically involves strict routines and schedules	Allows for flexible routines, emphasizes rhythm over a rigid schedule
Respect for Individuality	Focuses on conforming to societal norms and expectations	Respects and celebrates a child's individuality, nurturing unique strengths and interests
Emotional Expression	May discourage open emotional expression or encourage suppressing feelings	Encourages open emotional expression and provides a safe space for children to express their feelings

How does Traditional Parenting & Waldorf Inspired Parenting impact certain aspects of the child future?

Aspect	Traditional Parenting	Waldorf Parenting
Academic Focus	Early emphasis on academic achievement, grades, and performance.	A balanced approach that values experiential learning, creativity, and holistic development.
Compliance	Encourages children to conform to societal norms and expectations.	Fosters independent thinking, creativity, and critical problem-solving.
Emphasis on Technology	Often includes early exposure to screens and technology.	Limited use of technology, with a focus on imaginative play and real-world experiences.
Resilience	Children may or may not develop resilience skills.	Encourages resilience and adaptability through experiential learning and problem-solving.
Nature Connection	May or may not prioritize a connection to nature.	Promotes a strong connection to nature and the environment.
Emotional Intelligence	Emotional expression and understanding may vary.	Encourages emotional intelligence and provides a safe space for emotional expression.
Future Impact	Can lead to high academic achievements but may induce stress and external validation seeking.	Nurtures well-rounded individuals with creative and critical thinking skills, emotional intelligence, and a connection to nature.

How does Waldorf-inspired parenting address common mistakes often made in traditional parenting?

Common Mistakes in Traditional Parenting	How Waldorf-Inspired Parenting Addresses Them
Early Academic Pressure	Focuses on play, creativity, and imagination during early years.
Overuse of Technology	Advocates limited screen time and sensory experiences.
Competitive Nature	Promotes a non-competitive atmosphere and values individual development.
Over-scheduling	Balances structured activities with free play and nature exploration.
Materialism	Prioritizes meaningful experiences, relationships, and inner well-being.
Lack of Connection to Nature	Emphasizes outdoor exploration and environmental awareness.
Focus on Grades and Test Scores	Values a well-rounded education beyond academic assessments.
Parental Over-control	Encourages independence and responsibility within boundaries.
Lack of Emotional Expression	Provides a safe space for open emotional expression and emotional awareness.
One-Size-Fits-All Approach	Tailors parenting techniques to the unique needs of each child.

Disciplining the Child

Disciplining a child is a nuanced and crucial dimension of parenting. It isn't about asserting control or resorting to punitive measures; instead, it serves as a means to mentor and impart vital life skills to children, helping them navigate life's intricacies. Traditionally, methods like shouting, yelling, instilling fear, and even physical punishment have been employed by parents as disciplinary tools.

The impact of shouting, yelling, instilling fear, and resorting to physical punishment on a child's future can be profound and largely negative. These harsh disciplinary methods, often employed in traditional parenting, can lead to various detrimental consequences for the child's development, both in the short and long term. The child's emotional, psychological, and social well-being may be significantly affected.

An overview of the potential adverse outcomes on the child are as follow: -

1. **Emotional Distress:** Shouting, yelling, and the fear of physical punishment can result in emotional distress for the child. They may experience anxiety, low self-esteem, and a persistent fear of authority figures.

2. **Aggressive Behaviour:** Children subjected to aggressive disciplinary tactics may internalize these behaviours. As a result, they might become more prone to aggression and hostility, both in their interpersonal relationships and in how they handle conflicts.

3. **Communication Issues:** Constant exposure to yelling and shouting can hinder the child's ability to communicate effectively. They might struggle with expressing their thoughts and emotions, resorting to avoidance or confrontational behaviour instead.

4. **Low Self-Esteem:** Harsh discipline can erode a child's self-esteem. They may develop feelings of inadequacy and a negative self-image, which can persist into adulthood and affect their self-confidence.

5. **Trust Issues:** Instilling fear and using physical punishment can lead to trust issues in the child. They might find it challenging to trust others and develop healthy, positive relationships.

6. **Mental Health Implications:** These disciplinary methods can contribute to various mental health issues, such as depression, anxiety, and even post-traumatic stress disorder (PTSD).

7. **Academic Impact:** The child's performance in school can be negatively affected. They may struggle with concentration, focus, and motivation, leading to academic underachievement.

8. **Rebellion and Defiance:** Some children subjected to harsh discipline may become more rebellious and defiant. They may resent authority and act out against rules and expectations.

9. **Cycle of Abuse:** Research suggests that children who experience physical punishment are more likely to perpetuate the cycle of abuse in their own parenting practices in the future.

Waldorf-inspired approach focus on understanding the child's developmental stage, offering guidance and boundaries through empathetic and nurturing methods. The Waldorf-inspired approach aims to foster a strong sense of self, emotional well-being, and resilience, contributing to a more positive and harmonious future.

It's crucial for parents to recognize the potential long-term consequences of harsh disciplinary tactics and opt for more compassionate, holistic methods to support their child's development.

In the realm of "Waldorf Inspired Parenting, the core tenet emphasizes the cultivation of a deep emotional connection with the child. Within this philosophy, empathy is regarded as the foundational element of effective discipline. It involves understanding the child's emotions, discerning their needs, and embracing their unique perspective to effectively guide their behavior. Some recommended solutions are:-

- **Setting Realistic Boundaries:** While championing empathy and understanding, this approach also recognizes the importance of establishing rational limits. Parents are encouraged to communicate these boundaries clearly and consistently, all while tailoring them to the child's developmental stage and individual needs.

- **Embracing Rhythms and Predictability:** "Waldorf Inspired Parenting" advocates for the adoption of daily and weekly rhythms to create a secure and predictable environment for the child. The consistency of these routines helps children feel safe and supported.

- **Creating a Nurturing Environment:** This parenting approach underscores the significance of simplifying the child's surroundings by removing clutter and overwhelming stimuli. A simplified space can lead to a calmer and more focused child.

- **Teaching Self-Regulation:** Instead of relying on external rewards and punishments, "Waldorf Inspired Parenting" focuses on empowering children with self-regulation and decision-making skills. Parents guide their children in making choices and understanding the consequences of their actions.

- **Respect for Individuality:** The philosophy acknowledges that each child is unique, and their discipline should be tailored to their specific needs and temperament. Parents are encouraged to honor and respect a child's individuality.

- **Prioritizing Parental Self-Care:** "Waldorf Inspired Parenting" emphasizes the importance of self-care for parents. When parents take care of themselves, they are better equipped to provide the support and guidance that their children need for their holistic development.

Why Waldorf Education Hasn't Sparked a Global Movement Yet?

As we approach the final chapters of this enlightening journey, a question might stir in your thoughts - why, despite its remarkable depth and potency, has the paradigm of Waldorf education not yet reached the pinnacle of public recognition and fame?

The answer to this inquiry lies within the intricacies of the educational landscape.

Waldorf education, a gem cherished by those who have delved into its profound wisdom, remains somewhat concealed from the limelight. Several factors contribute to this veiled status, and understanding these aspects unveils the nuances of its journey.

1. **Relatively Recent Origin:** Waldorf education was founded in the early 20th century by Rudolf Steiner. It's a relatively recent educational philosophy compared to more traditional systems that have centuries of history. This has limited its time to gain widespread recognition.

2. **Alternative Approach:** Waldorf education takes a unique, holistic, and child-centered approach that may differ significantly from mainstream educational systems. This can make it less familiar to parents and educators.

3. **Limited Marketing:** Waldorf schools often prioritize education over marketing. They may not actively promote themselves or engage in advertising campaigns, which can limit their visibility.

4. **Smaller Network:** There are fewer Waldorf schools and institutions compared to public or private schools following traditional curricula. This smaller network naturally results in less widespread awareness.

5. **Educational Skepticism:** New or alternative educational approaches sometimes face skepticism or resistance, especially from those who are used to more conventional systems.

6. **Cultural Variations:** Waldorf education is not universally the same everywhere. Different schools and regions may adapt and interpret its principles in slightly different ways, which can lead to variations in its implementation.

7. **Misconceptions:** There may be misconceptions or misunderstandings about Waldorf education, which affects its reputation.

8. **Philosophy and Approach:** Waldorf Education is based on the anthroposophical philosophy of Rudolf Steiner, which includes spiritual and esoteric elements. While this philosophy resonates with many parents and educators, it may also be seen as unconventional or less familiar to others, leading to some hesitation in embracing it.

9. **Limited Resources:** Waldorf schools often require dedicated teachers and a specific curriculum, which can be more resource-intensive than traditional education systems. As a result, it may be challenging for some communities to establish and maintain Waldorf schools.

10. **Accreditation and Recognition:** In some countries, Waldorf Education may face challenges in obtaining government accreditation and recognition, which can affect its growth and acceptance as a mainstream educational option.

11. **Parental Awareness:** Many parents may not be familiar with the principles and benefits of Waldorf Education, leading them to choose more well-established and conventional schooling options for their children. This is the key pointer which is why we are writing this book.

12. **Teacher Training:** Waldorf Education requires teachers to undergo specialized training to fully understand and implement its unique principles. Ensuring a consistent level of teacher training and expertise across different regions can be a challenge.

Nevertheless, Waldorf education stands as a testament to the persistence of a dedicated community of parents, teachers, and individuals who wholeheartedly embrace its principles. Their unwavering commitment to nurturing a holistic, child-centric approach to learning embodies the spirit of Waldorf Education, and their advocacy continues to disseminate its timeless wisdom.

While the journey of Waldorf education may be an unconventional path, it is, in essence, a voyage towards fostering well-rounded individuals who appreciate the profound connection between knowledge, creativity, and humanity. The road less traveled often reveals the most magnificent landscapes, and the wisdom imparted by Waldorf education is a treasure worth unearthing.

What can we as parents/supporters do spread the word about Waldorf Education?

As Waldorf parents/supporters/admirers, there are several actions you can take to spread the word about Waldorf education and help others understand its value:

1. **Engage in Open Dialogue:** Have open conversations with friends, family, and acquaintances about your child's experiences in a Waldorf school. Share what you appreciate about the Waldorf approach and its impact on your child.

2. **Organize Information Sessions:** Host informal gatherings or information sessions where you invite interested parents to learn more about Waldorf education. You can share your personal experiences and invite Waldorf teachers or representatives to speak.

3. **Utilize Social Media:** Create or join social media groups and platforms dedicated to Waldorf education. Share articles, videos, and personal anecdotes about the benefits of Waldorf, and engage with questions and discussions.

4. **Support Your School:** Actively participate in your school's outreach efforts. Many Waldorf schools organize open houses and events. Offer to help organize or volunteer during these occasions.

5. **Write Blogs or Articles:** If you enjoy writing, consider starting a blog or contributing articles to local publications about Waldorf education, your experiences, and its principles. This can reach a broader audience.

6. **Demonstrate Your Child's Growth:** Waldorf education often focuses on the holistic development of children. Share examples of your child's growth, creativity, and well-being. People are often convinced by real-life examples.

7. **Attend Fairs and Exhibitions:** Participate in local education fairs or community events to represent Waldorf schools. Set up a booth and provide information to interested parents.

8. **Recommend Waldorf Books:** Suggest books and resources that explain the philosophy and practices of Waldorf education. Offer these recommendations to parents who want to learn more.

9. **Offer to Give Tours:** Volunteer to give school tours to prospective parents. Sharing your perspective as a Waldorf parent can be very enlightening for those considering Waldorf for their children.

10. **Foster Inclusivity:** Emphasize how Waldorf education celebrates diversity and inclusion. Highlight how Waldorf schools aim to create a nurturing environment for all children, regardless of their backgrounds or abilities.

11. **Join Parent Associations:** Many Waldorf schools have parent associations. Actively participate and collaborate with other parents to strengthen the school community and its visibility.

12. **Support the Arts:** Emphasize the importance of arts in Waldorf education. Attend school performances, art shows, and musical events. Share these experiences with others to showcase the creativity nurtured in Waldorf schools.

Let it be known that your fervor and heartfelt devotion to the ideals of Waldorf education possess the power to ignite the flames of inspiration in the hearts of others. As you share the depths of your enthusiasm and the tapestry of your personal experiences, you become a beacon, casting a radiant light of awareness and kindling the fires of interest within your circle of friends and throughout your community.

Your passion is the elixir that can transcend boundaries, connecting hearts and minds to the profound philosophy that is Waldorf. With each story you tell, with each anecdote you weave, you are painting a vivid mural of the Waldorf journey, inviting others to step into this enchanted realm of holistic learning.

In your earnest endeavors, you embody the spirit of Waldorf education, a spirit that recognizes the immense potential in every child, the boundless creativity within each soul, and the importance of nurturing the innate connection between humanity, wisdom, and the world we inhabit.

Like a fragrant blossom that spreads its perfume to the winds, your words and experiences have the potential to touch and transform lives, leaving an indelible mark of curiosity and reverence for the path of Waldorf. Your story is a testament to the profound change that can transpire when one embraces the philosophy, practices, and principles that underpin this unique educational journey.

So, let your voice resonate, let your tales inspire, and let your authentic passion become the catalyst that kindles the fires of curiosity, paving the way for others to embark on their own wondrous expedition into the realm of Waldorf education.

13 Waldorf Schools in India: A Deeper Exploration

The movement began in the year 1997 when the first Waldorf school in India, Sloka Waldorf School, was established in Hyderabad in 1997- Sloka Waldorf School opened its doors in Hyderabad with approximately 19 children and 4 teachers (As per information available on internet). Since then, the concept of holistic education has been slowly but steadily spreading across the country. It's important to note that Waldorf education in India is not confined to a specific region; schools and kindergartens have emerged in various states and some remote villages, reflecting the growing acceptance and recognition of this unique educational philosophy.

Demographics and Social Inclusivity:

One of the notable aspects of Waldorf schools in India is their diversity. These institutions cater to students from a wide range of socio-economic backgrounds and cultural contexts. Waldorf education's principles of inclusivity and individualized learning have contributed to the appeal of these schools across different communities.

Holistic Approach in Indian Context:

The Waldorf approach to education resonates well with the Indian context, where the demand for holistic, value-based education is on the rise. The emphasis on nurturing not only academic skills but also emotional intelligence, artistic expression, and moral values aligns with the expectations of Indian parents and educators. Many parents in India are seeking educational alternatives that prioritize the overall well-being and character development of their children.

Cultural Integration:

While Waldorf schools worldwide adhere to certain common principles, they also have the flexibility to incorporate local cultural elements. In India, this manifests in the incorporation of Indian festivals, traditions, and stories into the curriculum. This cultural integration is more than just an add-on; it's an essential part of the educational experience. It ensures that students maintain a strong connection to their cultural heritage while benefiting from the holistic approach of Waldorf education.

Artistic Expression and Cognitive Development:

Research in the Indian context has shown that the emphasis on artistic expression in Waldorf education has a positive impact on cognitive development. Activities such as painting, music, and eurythmy not only enhance creativity but also contribute to cognitive skills, emotional regulation, and social development. These activities are recognized as valuable tools for fostering a well-rounded and balanced education.

Community and Parental Involvement:

Waldorf schools in India place significant importance on building a sense of community. Students, teachers, and parents often come together to create a supportive and inclusive environment. Parental involvement is encouraged through various activities, including festivals, meetings, and collaborative projects. This strong sense of community fosters a shared responsibility for the education and well-being of the children.

Challenges and Opportunities:

As Waldorf education in India continues to grow, it faces certain challenges. These include the need for more qualified Waldorf teachers, resources for infrastructure development, and broader recognition within mainstream educational systems.

These challenges are being addressed through various initiatives:

- **Waldorf Teacher Training Programs:** India has seen the establishment of Waldorf teacher training programs aimed at producing more qualified Waldorf educators. These programs focus on the specific pedagogy and principles of Waldorf education, ensuring that teachers are well-prepared to deliver an authentic Waldorf experience.

- **Recognition and Awareness:** Efforts are underway to raise awareness about Waldorf education in India. Advocacy groups, educators, and parents are working together to promote the benefits of holistic education. As awareness grows, the hope is that more parents and educators will choose Waldorf education for its unique approach.

While Waldorf education in India is still in its nascent stages, it holds tremendous potential. Research conducted in India and globally has consistently shown the positive impact of Waldorf education on students' cognitive, emotional, and social development. As this approach continues to gain recognition and support, we can expect more Waldorf schools to emerge, offering students an education that nurtures not only academic skills but also the qualities that make them well-rounded individuals. In the coming years, as the demand for holistic education grows, Waldorf schools in India are likely to play a significant role in shaping the country's educational landscape.

List of Waldorf schools in India

Each of these schools embodies the spirit and ethos of Waldorf education, creating spaces where children can blossom, explore, and thrive in a holistic, artistic, and nurturing environment. It is a beautiful tapestry that reflects the profound impact of Waldorf-inspired education in the diverse landscape of India.

Sr. No.	School Name	Location	City
1	Shining Spiral Ahmedabad	Vejalpur	Ahmedabad
2	Prakriti, A Waldorf Kindergarten	Indiranagar	Bengaluru
3	Advaya Shaale	Kasturi Nagar	Bengaluru
4	TALC	Kundalahalli	Bengaluru
5	Tulasi Waldorf Kindergarten	Kengeri	Bengaluru
6	Promise Centre Waldorf Kindergarten	Babusapalya	Bengaluru
7	InBloom Waldorf Kindergarten	Domlur	Bengaluru
8	Kingdom of Childhood	JP Nagar	Bengaluru
9	Bangalore Steiner School	Hobli	Ramanagara, Bidadi
10	The Chennai Waldorf School	Neelankarai	Chennai
11	Indradhanu Waldorf School	Nungambakkam	Chennai
12	The Vels Academy	SKP Gardens	Erode

Sr. No.	School Name	Location	City
13	Swechha Waldorf Inspired School	Rushikonda	Gandhi Nagar
14	Sloka–The Hyderabad Waldorf School	Jubilee Hills	Hyderabad
15	Abhaya - a Waldorf School	Kompally	Hyderabad
16	Prerana Waldorf School	Janardana Hills	Hyderabad
17	Diksha - A Waldorf School	Shamirpet	Hyderabad
18	Uday Waldorf Inspired School	Tonk road	Jaipur
19	Inodai Waldorf School	Marol, Andheri East	Mumbai
20	Mumbai Waldorf Kindergarten	Goregaon West	Mumbai
21	Tridha	Andheri East	Mumbai
22	Kalpavruksha	Chembur	Mumbai
23	Nagpur Waldorf Inspired School	Ramdaspeth	Nagpur
24	Shishyaa Waldorf School	Vashi	Navi Mumbai
25	Aarambh Waldorf School	Vasant Kunj	New Delhi
26	Aritram Waldorf	Noida	Noida
27	Ukti - The Delhi Waldorf School	Noida	Noida
28	Banyan Steiner School	Noida	Noida
29	Swadhaa Waldorf Learning Centre	Pashan	Pune
30	Bonafide Waldorf inspired Kindergarten	Sivanandam	Thrissur
31	Lokhaa- A Waldorf Inspired School	Dharapuram	Tiruppur
32	Veda Vyas School	Bogigoundendasarapatti	Tiruppur
33	Swechha	Rushikonda	Visakhapatnam

Note: While every effort has been made to compile a comprehensive list of Waldorf-inspired schools in India, it is important to note that the information provided is based on research from publicly available sources on the internet. There may be additional schools in India that follow the Waldorf educational philosophy which are not included in this list. The absence of any school from this list does not imply any judgment or assessment of the quality or authenticity of their educational approach. This list is not an endorsement of the any of the above schools, nor do we have any personal reference or experience regarding the quality of education they provide. Readers are encouraged to conduct their own research and verification when seeking information about Waldorf-inspired schools in India, and this list should serve as a general reference guide. Please verify your information and details while seeking admissions or dealing with the schools. Please pardon us and we apologize if we have missed some names. We are not responsible for any matters related to the above schools.

Reference Point: You may refer to https://siwka.org/ Sadhana, the Indian Waldorf kindergartens association website for some details of schools.

Our highest endeavour must be to develop free human beings who are able of themselves to impart purpose and direction to their lives. The need for imagination, a sense of truth, and a feeling of responsibility — these three forces are the very nerve of education

– Rudolf Steiner

Thank You

In the enchanting tapestry of Waldorf education, the radiant journey of young Arnav emerges as a heartwarming tale, painting strokes of inspiration on the canvas of remarkable children. Arnav is not merely a student at Big Waldorf School; he embodies the very soul of Waldorf's pledge to honor the individuality and unique needs of each child.

Embarking on his odyssey at the illustrious Big Waldorf School, Arnav found not just a place of learning but a sanctuary of acceptance and understanding. Here, he wasn't singled out; instead, he was embraced as any other child, for Waldorf education dances to the rhythm of celebrating the distinctive qualities that render every child extraordinary. Arnav's needs took center stage in his educational voyage, crafting an environment where he could not just learn but thrive, nurtured by the school's unwavering commitment.

Arnav's transformative sojourn at the New Big Waldorf School was a testament to the school's recognition of his untapped potential. It wasn't about making adjustments; it was about sculpting a learning haven that would allow each child to bloom in their own unique way. This, dear reader, encapsulates the very essence of Waldorf education—an ode to individualized growth and flourishing.

As we revel in the pages of "Sarvavyaapi Siksha," Arnav's narrative stands as a living testament to the inclusive and compassionate spirit echoing through the corridors of Waldorf Education. His journey serves as a poignant reminder that when a community unites to nurture every child, extraordinary odysseys of growth and inclusion unfold.

With profound appreciation to the Waldorf School and the tireless efforts they continue to pour into shaping these transformative narratives, the pages of "Sarvavyaapi Siksha" gracefully turn, reaching the final chapter. To each cherished reader who embarked on this educational odyssey, we extend our heartfelt gratitude.

Education, we believe, is a majestic journey, and together, we have explored the transformative magic that Waldorf education weaves. As we take our final steps in this literary ballet, we extend our deepest thanks for your unyielding support, insatiable curiosity, and dedication to the cause of holistic education.

May the words within these pages not merely be letters on paper but sparks that kindle a fervor for nurturing the boundless potential in every child and for creating a world of inclusive, compassionate learning. Together, hand in hand, let us paint a brighter tomorrow for the cherished children of today.

With deepest appreciation and warmest regards,

Diptii Karaambe & Ameya V Karrambe

Top 50 FAQ's on Waldorf Education

1. What is Waldorf education?

   - Waldorf education is a holistic and child-centered approach to learning developed by Rudolf Steiner. It focuses on nurturing a child's intellectual, emotional, and physical development.

2. Who is Rudolf Steiner?

   - Rudolf Steiner was an Austrian philosopher and educator who founded the Waldorf education system in the year an around 1919, A hundred years on, the Waldorf education movement has burgeoned into an independent school movement. It may have around 1,000+ independent schools, nearly 2,000+ kindergartens spanning across 75 countries, and an additional 500+ special education centers flourishing in over 40 countries.

3. What is the Waldorf curriculum based on?

   - The Waldorf curriculum is based on the stages of child development and emphasizes the arts, practical skills, and experiential learning.

4. Are Waldorf schools religious?

   - Waldorf schools are not tied to any specific religion. They are non-denominational and welcome students of all backgrounds.

5. What is the role of teachers in Waldorf education?

   - Waldorf teachers act as guides, mentors, and facilitators. They aim to inspire a love for learning in their students.

6. Do Waldorf schools use textbooks and standardized testing?

    o Waldorf schools typically avoid standardized tests and textbooks. They prefer experiential learning and create their own materials.

7. What are the main principles of Waldorf education?

    o Key principles include child-centered learning, a focus on arts and creativity, and an emphasis on experiential learning.

8. Are there Waldorf schools in India?

    o Yes, there are several Waldorf schools in India, with a growing presence in different regions.

9. How do Waldorf schools differ from traditional schools?

    o Waldorf schools emphasize holistic education, experiential learning, and creativity, whereas traditional schools often rely on textbooks and standardized testing.

10. What is the Waldorf philosophy on technology and screen time?

    o Waldorf schools limit the use of technology and screens for young children and believe that hands-on experiences are more valuable.

11. What age group do Waldorf schools serve?

    o Waldorf schools typically serve children from preschool through high school.

12. Are there homework assignments in Waldorf schools?

    o Waldorf schools aim to keep homework minimal, especially in the early years. They prioritize learning during school hours.

13. What subjects are taught in Waldorf schools?

   ○ Waldorf schools cover a wide range of subjects, including traditional academics, the arts, and practical skills.

14. Is Waldorf education expensive?

   ○ Tuition fees at Waldorf schools can vary, but they are often on par with or slightly below other private schools.

15. Can children with special needs attend Waldorf schools?

   ○ Some Waldorf schools are equipped to support children with special needs, while others may have limited resources in this regard.

16. How do Waldorf schools assess students' progress?

   ○ Waldorf schools use narrative assessments, observations, and evaluations of student work instead of traditional grades and standardized tests.

17. Do Waldorf schools teach languages and sports?

   ○ Yes, Waldorf schools offer language instruction and include sports and physical education in their curriculum.

18. What is the Waldorf approach to early childhood education?

   ○ Waldorf early childhood programs focus on nurturing a child's imagination and creativity through play and artistic activities.

19. What is the role of art and creativity in Waldorf education?

   ○ Art, music, and creative activities are integral to Waldorf education, as they stimulate a child's imagination and cognitive development.

20. How do Waldorf schools foster a connection to nature?

    o Waldorf schools often incorporate outdoor education and nature-based activities to encourage a love for the natural world.

21. Are there Waldorf teacher training programs?

    o Yes, Waldorf teacher training programs are available for individuals interested in becoming Waldorf educators.

22. Do Waldorf schools follow a strict daily routine?

    o Waldorf schools usually have a consistent daily rhythm that includes artistic and practical activities.

23. Can parents become actively involved in Waldorf schools?

    o Parents are encouraged to participate in their child's education, engage with the school community, and volunteer.

24. Are there Waldorf high schools?

    o Yes, there are Waldorf high schools that continue the holistic and arts-based approach to education.

25. Is Waldorf education suitable for gifted children?

    o Waldorf education can be adapted to meet the needs of gifted children, as it values individualized learning.

26. What are the main criticisms of Waldorf education?

    o Critics may argue that the lack of standardized testing and the emphasis on experiential learning can be a drawback in today's competitive world.

27. How do Waldorf schools address diversity and inclusion?

    o Waldorf schools aim to create inclusive environments, but they may face challenges in terms of diversity and access.

28. Can children transition from Waldorf schools to traditional schools?

    o   Yes, children can transition to traditional schools if needed, but they may require an adjustment period.

29. Is there a Waldorf curriculum for homeschooling?

    o   Yes, there are Waldorf-inspired homeschooling curricula available for parents who prefer to educate their children at home.

30. Are Waldorf schools associated with anthroposophy?

    o   Waldorf education has its roots in anthroposophy, but it is non-denominational and not religious.

31. Do Waldorf schools have a uniform dress code?

    o   Waldorf schools generally do not have strict uniform dress codes and often allow comfortable, simple clothing.

32. How does Waldorf education address bullying and discipline?

    o   Waldorf schools prioritize creating a respectful and supportive environment to address issues of bullying and discipline.

33. What is the role of fairy tales and mythology in Waldorf education?

    o   Fairy tales and mythology are often used as teaching tools to engage students' imaginations and moral development.

34. Are there Waldorf schools in rural areas?

    o   Yes, Waldorf schools can be found in both urban and rural areas, offering a unique educational option to diverse communities.

35. What is the Waldorf perspective on standardized testing and grades?

   o   Waldorf schools emphasize the holistic development of students and may avoid traditional grading systems and standardized testing.

36. How do Waldorf schools approach technology education?

   o   Waldorf schools may introduce technology education in later grades but emphasize experiential learning and limit screen time.

37. Can adults receive Waldorf education or training?

   o   Yes, Waldorf teacher training programs and workshops are available for adults interested in Waldorf education.

38. How do Waldorf schools promote social and emotional development?

   o   Waldorf schools focus on building strong social and emotional foundations through community, art, and experiential learning.

39. What is the Waldorf perspective on homework?

   o   Waldorf schools aim to keep homework minimal, especially in the early years, to allow time for play, exploration, and creativity.

40. How do Waldorf schools celebrate festivals and seasons?

   o   Waldorf schools often mark the changing seasons and celebrate festivals with music, art, and cultural activities.

41. Is there a specific teacher-student ratio in Waldorf schools?

   o   Waldorf schools typically maintain low teacher-student ratios to allow for individualized attention.

42. How are Waldorf teachers trained?

    o Waldorf teachers undergo specialized training programs, including coursework in anthroposophy and child development.

43. What role does music play in Waldorf education?

    o Music is integral to Waldorf education and is used to enhance emotional expression, creativity, and cognitive development.

44. Can children with learning disabilities thrive in Waldorf schools?

    o Some Waldorf schools provide additional support for children with learning disabilities, while others may have limited resources in this regard.

45. Do Waldorf schools provide religious or moral education?

    o Waldorf schools aim to nurture a child's sense of ethics and morality but are non-denominational and non-religious.

46. How are Waldorf schools funded?

    o Waldorf schools are typically funded through tuition, fundraising, donations, and grants.

47. What is the impact of Waldorf education on children's creativity?

    o Waldorf education is designed to stimulate a child's imagination and foster creative thinking.

48. What is the role of storytelling in Waldorf education?

    o Storytelling is used to engage students' imagination and language development, as well as to convey lessons and values.

49. What is the Waldorf approach to early reading and writing?

   o Waldorf schools often delay formal reading and writing instruction, focusing on developing language skills through storytelling and listening.

50. Are there Waldorf Education boards?

   o Yes, there are Waldorf Education boards that offer programs affiliation.

Our Suggestions to Read

1. Simplicity Parenting: Using the Extraordinary Power of Less to Raise Calmer, Happier, and More Secure Kids

2. The Soul of Discipline: The Simplicity Parenting Approach to Warm, Firm, and Calm Guidance- From Toddlers to Teens

3. Being at Your Best When Your Kids Are at Their Worst: Practical Compassion in Parenting

4. Autism: Meet Me Who I Am by Dr. Lakshmi Prasanna and Michael Kokinos

5. Stop Parenting, Start Gardening: Relaxed Parents, Joyful Children- Bindu Chowdary

6. Beyond the Rainbow Bridge: Nurturing Our Children from Birth to Seven-Barbara J. Patterson

7. The Kingdom of Childhood: Introductory Talks on Waldorf Education- Steiner

8. Understanding Waldorf Education: Teaching from the Inside Out by Jack Petrash

9. Seven Times the Sun: Guiding Your Child Through the Rhythms of the Day- by Shea Darian

10. Too Much Too Soon: Early Learning and the Erosion of Childhood- Richard House

11. Meeting the Child in Steiner Kindergartens: An exploration of beliefs, values and practices- Ed R. Parker-Rees

12. Educating through Art: the Steiner School Approach. Agnes Nobel

13. Education Towards Freedom F. Carlgren

14. Genius of Play- Sally Jenkinson

15. Rudolf Steiner Education – An Introductory Reader Christopher Clouder

16. School as a Journey- Torin M Finser.

17. Waldorf Education- Christopher Clouder, Martyn Rawson

18. You are Your Child's First Teacher- Rahima Baldwin Dancy.

19. Teaching as a Lively Art: Marjorie Spock.

Some Recommended Courses

1. IRA Teacher Training – https://www.iralearn.com/

2. CSETT – https://www.inodai.com/

3. Most waldorf schools conduct programs for parents & new teacher development

4. Siwka – http://www.siwka.org/

5. Simplicity Parenting – https://www.simplicityparenting.com/trainings

Our Favorite Reads

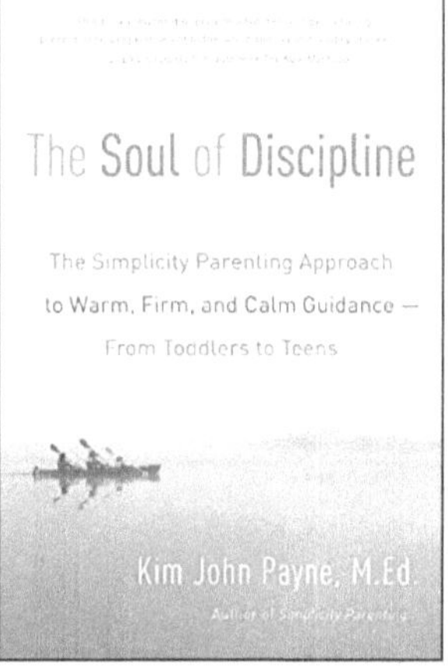

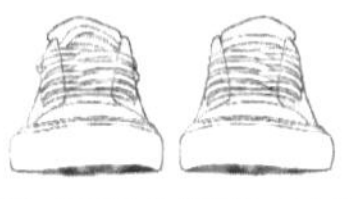

Where is the book in which the teacher can read about what teaching is? The children themselves are this book. We should not learn to teach out of any book other than the one lying open before us and consisting of the children themselves.

– Rudolf Steiner

Author's Disclaimer

This book, "Sarvavyaapi Shiksha: Harmonizing Growth and Inclusion for Every Child," is a work of research, insights, and experiences aimed at promoting awareness about holistic education, especially within the context of Waldorf education principles. As authors, we want to clarify that we are not responsible for any actions taken by readers based on the information presented in this book.

The content within these pages is not intended as professional advice, and it does not offer prescriptions for specific actions or decisions. The information provided is based on research, educational philosophy, and personal experiences, and its applicability may vary across different situations.

Readers are strongly urged to seek professional guidance and consult with relevant experts, such as medical professionals, and specialists, to address specific concerns or conditions related to children's health, development, or education. The authors disclaim any liability arising directly or indirectly from the use of information provided in this book.

It is important to recognize that every child is unique, and their needs are diverse. This book does not substitute for individualized advice tailored to specific circumstances. The experiences shared in this book are anecdotal and may not encompass the full range of individual experiences within the realm of Waldorf education.

We encourage readers to approach the content critically, consider various perspectives, and engage in further research to make well-informed decisions. Our intent is to inspire thoughtful discussions, reflections, and a deeper understanding of holistic education.

In essence, as authors, we want to emphasize that readers assume responsibility for their interpretations of the content and any actions taken as a result. The book is a tool for awareness and discussion, and individual circumstances may warrant seeking personalized and professional advice.